Question and Answer

Oviedo Hangman

1987

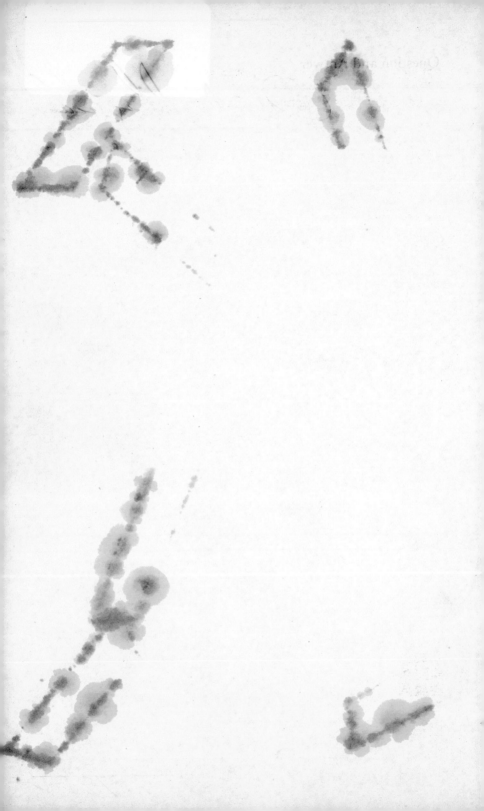

QUESTION AND ANSWER
Graded Oral Comprehension Exercises

L. G. ALEXANDER

New Edition
Revised by PETER FERGUSON

LONGMAN

LONGMAN GROUP LIMITED
Longman House
Burnt Mill, Harlow, Essex, U.K.

This edition first published 1977

Fourth impression 1981

ISBN 0 582 55206 0

Printed in Singapore by
Selector Printing Co Pte Ltd

Also by LG Alexander

Language Practice Books:
Sixty Steps to Précis
Poetry and Prose Appreciation for
    Overseas Students
Essay and Letter-writing
A First Book in Comprehension,
    Précis and Composition
Reading and Writing English
Guided Composition in English
    Language Teaching
In Other Words

I Think You Think:
    30 Discussion Topics for Adults
Make Your Point:
    30 Discussion Topics for
    Students at Secondary Level
For and Against

**The Carters of Greenwood
    (Cineloops):**
Teacher's Handbook
Elementary Workbook
Intermediate Workbook

Look, Listen and Learn:
Pupils' Books 1–4
Teacher's Books 1–4
Workbooks-Link Readers

New Concept English:
First Things First
Practice and Progress
Developing Skills
Fluency in English

Mainline
Progress A & B
Skills A & B
Students' and Teacher's Books etc.

Target 1–3
Pupils' and Teacher's Books etc.

**Longman Structural Readers,
    Stage 1:**
Detectives from Scotland Yard
Car Thieves
Mr Punch
Operation Janus

**Longman Structural Readers,
    Stage 2:**
April Fools' Day
Worth a Fortune
Professor Boffin's Umbrella
K's First Case

**Longman Structural Readers,
    Stage 3:**
Operation Mastermind
Good morning, Mexico!
Dangerous Game
Clint Magee

**Longman Integrated
    Comprehension and
    Composition Series:**
    General Editor

Tell Us a Story

CONTENTS

Introduction

THE FOUNDATIONS OF SPEECH

The great majority of overseas students learning English are primarily interested in speaking the language. Paradoxically, such is the tyranny of the written word, they often get little opportunity to do so. In most English courses, far more attention is paid to writing than to speech. This is especially true for students who are preparing for examinations. Faced with the pressing requirements of an examination syllabus, teachers are often obliged to spend very little time on oral English. They work through a course in the conscious knowledge that their students will more or less have to bluff their way through an oral examination. Yet, ultimately, the student's knowledge of English will be judged by the world at large not on his capacity to write the language but to speak it.

As far as the teacher is concerned, part of the difficulty arises from the fact that lessons in conversation are not at all easy to conduct. Each lesson must be carefully prepared, otherwise the teacher will get little or no response from his class. No teacher would expect his students to attempt written composition before they had mastered a large number of basic sentence patterns and learnt to write simple, compound, and complex sentences. Yet he will often embark on a discussion with a class without providing his students with any prior training. Unprepared discussion on subjects like 'The Cinema Today' often lead nowhere and add nothing to the student's knowledge of the English language. During discussions of this sort, the student will often struggle painfully to express complex ideas in English. The teacher may be reluctant to correct him because this will interrupt the flow of conversation. Even if he does correct him, the student will retain very little. Sometimes the whole lesson breaks down and the teacher ends up doing all the talking. At other times, the conversation may prove to be so interesting that the students abandon English altogether and discuss the topic in their mother tongue.

Learning to speak a foreign language has much in common with learning to play a musical instrument. In each case, the final objective is that the student should be able to perform in public, making as few mistakes as possible. No one learning to play a musical instrument could possibly undertake to perform a difficult composition before he had mastered a large number of drills and exercises. The purpose behind these drills and exercises is that the student should ultimately be able to play with a minimum of error. In the same way, careful and methodical oral training is necessary long before it is possible for a language student to join in a discussion of a topic of general interest. If the student is asked to take part in a discussion without adequate preparation, he is being encouraged to make mistakes. He will ultimately adopt bad speech habits which may prove impossible to eradicate.

The method for oral training adopted in this book is based on carefully graded questions and answers. A full explanation is given in the Foreword to the Teacher. All the questions to be asked are closely related to a context so that the student's response will never be purely mechanical.

THE AIMS OF THIS BOOK
1 To train the student to understand spoken English.
2 To train the student to read aloud with correct stress and intonation.
3 To train the student to answer and to ask all types of questions and to establish the foundation of good speech habits.
4 To lead the student by stages to free oral expression so that he can take part in a discussion on topics of general interest.
5 To prepare the student adequately for the Cambridge First Certificate Examination.

LEVEL
This book may be begun by adult or secondary students who have been learning English for a year or less. It will bring them up to the level required by the Cambridge First Certificate Examination. Preferably, the book should be used as supplementary oral material to accompany any intermediate course. It may, for instance, be used effectively as a companion volume to *Practice and Progress* and *Developing Skills* and should be commenced after Unit One of *Practice and Progress* has been completed. The book should be used over a period of two years with students doing intensive courses, and over a period of four years with students learning English as part of a general curriculum.

ARRANGEMENT OF MATERIAL
Question and Answer contains six chapters each of which consists of eight passages followed by graded oral exercises. The book is prefaced by a

detailed introduction to teachers, outlining the methods employed. Each chapter is preceded by a summary of the question forms that can be used.

GRADING

The language content of Chapters 1–4 corresponds, with a small number of exceptions, with the Structural Tables which have been devised to accompany the Longmans' Structural Readers Series. Chapters 5 and 6 are more steeply graded to bring the student up to F.C.E. level. The whole emphasis has been on grading *structures* and *questions forms* rather than vocabulary. Each passage is situational, usually consisting of dialogue with connecting narrative, but is, at the same time, structurally controlled. This means that in each Chapter the student will be required to work within certain well-defined limits.

AUDIO MATERIAL

Each of the passages has been recorded on tape and is followed by fifteen mixed questions. Indication of how the mixed questions fit into the general scheme is given in the exercises that follow each passage. In Chapters 1–4, the speed of delivery begins at approximately 120 words per minute and is gradually increased. Pauses at natural breaks are longer than those which would be encountered in normal speech. These pauses may help the student to assimilate what he has heard. In Chapters 5 and 6, delivery is at normal speed. If the teacher has no tape-recorder, he may read the passages to the class, following the procedure suggested in the Foreword.

STRESS AND INTONATION MARKINGS

The passages in Chapters 1–5 are marked in such a way as to 'support' the tapes. The recorded texts follow the printed markings exactly. It must be emphasised that the markings are only an indication of the way the passages might be read, as obviously the pattern of stress in any statement is often a matter of opinion.

Complex systems of notation, forms of diagrammatic representation and phonetic symbols have been deliberately excluded, as they tend to confuse and intimidate overseas teachers and students, making the exercises look far more difficult than they really are. Only three marks have been used: the heavy stress mark: ´ (usually on nouns, verbs and adverbs) and two pause marks: / and //. The single stroke indicates a brief pause; the double stroke, a longer pause. Though these markings cannot possibly convey subtle variations in stress and intonation, they may help the student to read whole phrases rather than individual words. They will also serve to remind him of the reading he has heard on tape or from the teacher and thus provide him with sufficient information about the *sound* of each passage without encumbering him with a complex (and typographically unsightly) system of notation. Pause marks are not given in Chapter 1, as the printed statements in each passage do not exceed the learner's eye-span. The passages in Chapter 6 have not been marked in any way.

The value of reading aloud has been questioned by some linguists, as it is rightly claimed that a student of a foreign language is rarely if ever called upon to read aloud in a real-life situation. This is undoubtedly true. On the other hand, reading aloud may provide the student with extremely valuable practice in intonation. As Mr Roger Kingdon puts it in *English Intonation Practice*: 'Any weaknesses in intonation are particularly noticeable in reading aloud. In extempore speech one instinctively uses the stress and intonation that best convey one's meaning and express one's feelings, but in reading aloud one is attempting to render someone else's thought, and it is therefore less easy to find the right expression.'

THE NEW EDITION

While the essential features and objectives of *Question and Answer* remain unchanged, the new edition contains a number of modifications designed to bring the book into line with current theory and practice in oral teaching, while at the same time maintaining its effectiveness for First Certificate students. Changes are as follows:

1 The number of texts in each Chapter has been reduced from ten to eight to make room for the addition of new exercises.

2 Multiple Choice Comprehension Exercises relating to each text have been added (page 117) and a key provided (page 145).

3 Sixty brief descriptions of situations have been added (page 135) to provide opportunity to practise particular language functions. There are twenty such functions, each of which is recycled. Thus, Situations 1, 21 and 41 deal with 'accepting invitations' and so on. Situations 1–40 are labelled; 41–60 are unlabelled. Possible appropriate responses are supplied (page 141).

FOREWORD TO THE TEACHER
How to use this book

THE FORM OF EACH LESSON
A teacher is obviously free to use a book in any way that suits him best. The notes given below should be taken as suggestions only.

Each lesson may fall into seven parts, the last of which may be included at the discretion of the teacher:

1 Listening
2 Listening and Silent Reading
3 Reading Aloud
4 Listening and Understanding
5 Extensive Reading
6 Oral Exercises
7 Dictation

Two further stages may be added in the first ten lessons (Chapter 1). These are: Chorus Repetition and Individual Repetition. The two additional stages could come after Intensive Reading. The teacher should read the passage sentence by sentence and get the class to repeat each sentence after him, first in chorus, then individually. The students should not refer to their books when doing repetition work.

1 LISTENING
Aim: To give the student practice in listening to spoken English and understanding as much as possible of what he hears.
Procedure: Books shut. Play the recording or read the passage once without interruption. The students should listen only. At this stage, the students must not be allowed to listen to the recorded mixed questions which follow each passage.

2 LISTENING AND SILENT READING
Aim: To enable the student to match the sound of what he hears to the printed word.
Procedure: Books open. Play the recording through once or read the passage without interruption. The students should read silently while the recording is being played or the passage is being read. At this stage the students must not be allowed to listen to the recorded mixed questions which follow each passage.

3 INTENSIVE READING
Aim: To ensure that the students have understood what they have heard.

I

Procedure: Books open. The passage should be played or read to the class in small units. During each pause, explain unfamiliar words and constructions. Rather than give direct explanations, try to elicit as much information as possible from the students.

4 LISTENING AND UNDERSTANDING

Aim: To allow the students to hear the passage once more in the knowledge that they will now be in a position to understand it completely.

Procedure: Books shut. Play the recording or read the passage without interruption. The students should listen only. Again, the students must not be allowed to listen to the recorded mixed questions which follow each passage.

5 READING ALOUD

Aim: To enable the students to practise reading aloud with correct stress and intonation.

Procedure: Books open. In a single lesson, it will, of course, be impossible for *every* student in the class to read. Individual students should read about five lines of the passage at a time. While a student is reading, do not interrupt him. After he has completed his reading, comment (or, better still, get the class to comment) on the quality of stress, intonation and pronunciation. Phrases which have been read incorrectly should be repeated several times. The stress and pause marks should be observed as closely as possible. The students should be trained to read *whole phrases* rather than individual words.

Alternatively, groups of five or six students at a time may be asked to read in chorus. The combined effect is usually more correct than individual reading. Students can be trained, as members of an orchestra or choir can be trained, to listen to others while "playing" themselves.

6 ORAL EXERCISES

General Remarks

The oral exercises will form the main part of each lesson. The students should by now be sufficiently familiar with the passages to work with their books shut. On some occasions, however, the teacher may require the students to keep their books open so that they can refer to the printed version of a question when they have failed to understand it orally. The questions have been carefully graded to elicit particular types of response. The purpose of each exercise should be clearly explained to the students so that they fully understand what is required of them. Attention should be paid to the following:

Pace: During the first lessons, questions should be asked fairly slowly and the students should be given ample time to answer. Once the class has become thoroughly familiar with the techniques employed, the questions may be asked at a brisk pace. The student should be trained to give an accurate and automatic response to each question. The amount of time he is given to do this should be gradually reduced.

Pronoun changes: Where a passage is written in the first person, the student will be expected to identify himself with the character or characters taking part in the dialogue. This use of 'you' is slightly unrealistic in the circumstances, but cannot be avoided. Do not confine yourself to questions printed in the text. Where the printed questions aim at eliciting a third person response, supply questions which will elicit a first person response and vice versa.

Tense changes: The tenses used in the questions will be found to vary considerably. This may be a little confusing at first, but the intention has been to make the students listen very carefully to each question.

Complete and incomplete answers: In the past, teachers insisted on complete answers to all questions in the belief that this enabled the students to practise using verb forms. Full answers to questions, however, often amount to a complete distortion of natural speech. Students should be trained to give *natural* answers to all questions, that is, answers which would normally be expected.

For instance, if the question is:

Why did you leave at 4.0 o'clock?

The answer could be:

Because I had to go to the dentist.

Not:

I left at 4.0 o'clock because I had to go to the dentist.

More often than not, it is unnatural to incorporate part of the question in the answer.

Question grading: The questions following each passage have been graded as follows:

   A. *Yes and No Tag Answers* (All Chapters)

     Aim: To train the student to listen to the *first* word in each question and to use the *same* word in his answer. (There are a limited number of exceptions to this: e.g. *Are* you . . .? Yes, I am. Were you . . .? Yes, I was. There are certain instances, also, where a tag response would be impolite: e.g. Would you like to have dinner with us tomorrow? No, I wouldn't.)

Procedure: Explain the purpose of the exercise to the students. Tell them that you want them to listen to the *first* word in each question and to use the same word in their answers:

    Q. *Is* Miss Green in the library?
    A. Yes, she *is*.
    Q. *Can* you see her?
    A. No, I *can't*.

Where two types of tag answer are possible, the student should be trained to use both of them: e.g. No, he isn't, No, he's not; No, it isn't, No, it's not; No, I haven't, No, I've not; etc. In Chapters 5 and 6, the student should be trained to vary his tag answers:

    Q. *Isn't* it warm today?
    A. Yes, it *is*.
    A. Yes, it *is, isn't* it?
    A. Yes, *isn't* it?

B. *Questions with 'Who'* (All Chapters excluding Chapter 1)

    Aim: To train the student to supply the correct auxiliary verb in his answers.

Procedure: Explain that an auxiliary verb is often used in answer to questions beginning with *Who*. In most cases, the auxiliary verb is contained in the question (e.g. Who *is* . . .? Who *was* . . .?). When the question is in the simple present or simple past, however, the student must supply do/does/did in his answer:

    Q. Who *is* in the library?
    A. Miss Green *is*.
    Q. Who *likes* detective stories?
    A. I *do*. Mr Jones *does*.
    Q. Who went to the library yesterday?
    A. I *did*. Mr Jones *did*.

C. *Double Questions Joined by 'Or'* (All Chapters)

Aim: To train the student to give complete and accurate answers.

Procedure: Explain that the correct answer is contained in the question itself and that you want a complete answer to each question:

> Q. Did Inspector Jones go to the library or to the police station?
> A. He went to the library.

D. *Other Question Words* (All Chapters)

Aim: To elicit short or complete answers to general questions beginning with words like *When, Where, Why,* etc.

Procedure: Explain to the students that they should learn to associate a particular type of response with different question words:

> *What . . .?*—Short or complete answers:
> Q. What did you buy?
> A. A book.
> Q. What did he do?
> A. He went to the library.
> *Where . . .?*—Prepositions of place (at, in, on, etc.)
> Q. Where's Tom?
> A. (He's) in the garden.
> *Which . . .?*—Short answers often with *one* as a pronoun:
> Q. Which do you prefer?
> A. The blue one.
> Q. Which film did you see?
> A. Cleopatra.
> *Why . . .?*—because/to infinitive:
> Q. Why did he go to the library?
> A. Because he wanted to borrow a book.
> A. To borrow a book.
> *When . . .?*—Time phrases (yesterday, this morning, etc.); prepositions of time (at, on, in, etc.)
> Q. When did you first meet him?
> A. Last year.

Q. When is your appointment?
A. At 4.0 o'clock.
Q. When did you arrive?
A. On April 14th.
Whose . . .?—Possessive pronouns. Apostrophe 's'.
Q. Whose is this coat?
A. It's mine/Tom's.
How . . .?—Complete answers or *by* + *-ing*.
Q. How did you arrive at this figure?
A. I added up all these numbers.
A. By adding up all these numbers.
Who . . .? (in place of *Whom . . .?*)—Short answers:
Q. Who did you get this from?
A. My aunt.

E. *Mixed Questions* (All Chapters. Chapter 6 consists entirely of Mixed Questions)

Aim: To elicit the correct response to a variety of questions.

Procedure: These questions have been recorded after each passage. The recorded questions should be played to the class after the preceding exercises have been completed. The tape-recorder may be turned off after each recorded question is heard. There is a three second pause after each question.

F. *Asking Questions* (All Chapters)

Aim: To train the student to ask questions.

Procedure: The questions the student will ask are given in pairs. The student first asks a question using an auxiliary verb. Then he asks *precisely the same question again* preceding it with a question word:

Teacher: Ask me if he went out.
Student: Did he go out?
Teacher: Ask me when he went out.
Student: When *did he go out?*

Alternatively, the students may have their books open and ask each other questions.

G. *Extended Oral Exercises* (Chapters 4–6)

    Aim: To give the student practice in free oral expression.

Procedure: The following exercises have been given:

    1 *Imaginary Dialogues*

Two students at a time should conduct a dialogue based on information given in the passage. They should be encouraged to reproduce orally as many as they can of the phrases and expressions they have heard.

    2 *Oral Reproduction*

Two or three students should be given the opportunity to reproduce orally in reported speech the main ideas of the passage they have studied. To enable them to do this without stumbling, you may write key words and phrases on the blackboard to remind the students of the main sequence of events in the passage.

    3 *Free Discussion*

This exercise is introduced in Chapters 5 and 6 only. The subject matter for these discussions is related to material contained in each passage. Abstract and argumentative topics have been excluded. At this level, the student should be trained to make statements on everyday subjects (travel, careers, holidays, etc.).

Dictation

If there is time at the end of a lesson, two or three lines of dictation should be given from a passage that has already been studied. Dictations may be delivered by the students themselves.

THE NEW EDITION

Exercises added to the new edition (described on page 14 of the Introduction) may be exploited as follows:

MULTIPLE CHOICE COMPREHENSION

    Aim: To develop and test the students' ability to understand the texts.

    Procedure: Invite the students to tackle the multiple choice exercises (pages 117–133) relating to a particular text immediately after they have listened to it for the first time (Stage 1 of the Lesson). This gives them the opportunity to find out how much they can understand at first hearing and to practise trying to understand without explanation. Then invite the students to tackle the multiple choice exercises for a second time after Stage 4 (Listening and Understanding). Exercises may now be corrected and the key (page 145) may be consulted.

SITUATIONS

Aim: To give students the opportunity to practise making appropriate responses in a variety of social situations.

Procedure: The situations should be tackled parallel with Chapters 4–6: they may come at the end of each set of Oral Exercises (Stage 6 of the Lesson). Thus, Situations 1–20 should be introduced parallel with Chapter 4; 21–40 with Chapter 5 and 41–60 with Chapter 6.

Refer the students to a situation in their books (pages 135–140) and read the situation aloud. Make sure that each situation is completely understood by the class and the relationship of the speakers is clearly established. Now invite individual students to respond appropriately. Alternatively, invite pairs of students to take the parts described in each situation. Students may respond briefly or may use each situation as the basis for more extended role play and improvisation. Particular attention should be paid to the following: tone, manner and the appropriateness of socially acceptable forms in a given context. The possible appropriate responses (page 141) should be consulted only after the exercise has been finished: only the barest minimum is provided in this section.

Chapter 1

TO THE TEACHER

Summary of Question Forms

A. Yes and No Tag Answers

The following auxiliary verbs are used:

Am/is/are

Do/does

Can

B. Double questions joined by 'or'

C. Other question words

The only question word introduced here is *What*.

D. Mixed questions (Recorded)

E. Asking questions

PARTICULAR DIFFICULTIES

What colour . . .?

(What) am/is/are . . . going to . . .?

1   A Good Book

Inspéctor Róbert Jónes is a detéctive.
He líves near a líbrary.
Inspéctor Jónes is ín the líbrary nów.
He is tálking to Míss Gréen.

5   Míss Gréen is the librárian.

INSPECTOR JONES: Góod morning, Míss Gréen.
MISS GREEN: Good mórning, Inspéctor.
                    Cán I hélp you?
INSPECTOR JONES: Yés, you cán.
10   I am lóoking for a góod bóok.
MISS GREEN: Thís is a góod bóok, Inspéctor.
INSPECTOR JONES: What ís it?
MISS GREEN: It's a detéctive stóry.
INSPECTOR JONES: Góod! I líke detéctive stóries.
15   Whát's the múrderer's náme?
MISS GREEN: I cán't tell you thát, Inspéctor.
                    Í'm a librárian.
                    I'm nót a detéctive!

Answer these questions

A.   1 Is Robert Jones a detective?
       2 Is Robert Jones a librarian?
       3 Does Inspector Jones live near the library?
       4 Is Inspector Jones in the library now?
       5 Is Miss Green in the library too?
       6 Is Miss Green a librarian?
       7 Can she help the Inspector?
       8 Is the Inspector looking for a book?
       9 Can Miss Green give him a book?
    10 Is the book a detective story?
    11 Does the Inspector like detective stories?
    12 Does the Inspector know the murderer's name?
    13 Can Miss Green tell him the murderer's name?

B. 14 Is Robert Jones a detective or a librarian?
    15 Does he live near a library or near a school?
    16 Is Inspector Jones in the library or in his room?

17 Can Miss Green help the Inspector, or is she too busy?
18 Does the Inspector want a book or a newspaper?
19 Is the book good or bad?
20 Is the book a detective story, or is it a story about animals?

C. 21 What is the Inspector's name?
22 What is the librarian's name?
23 What does the Inspector want?
24 What is Miss Green?
25 What is Robert Jones?
26 What can Miss Green do?
27 What does the Inspector like?

D. Mixed questions (Recorded)

E. Ask these questions
Ask me
1a if Robert Jones is a detective.
b what he is.
2a if Miss Green is a librarian.
b what she is.
3a if the Inspector wants a book.
b what he wants.
4a if Miss Green can help him.
b what she can do.
5a if the Inspector likes detective stories.
b what the Inspector likes.
6a if Miss Green can tell him the murderer's name.
b what Miss Green can tell him.

2 In the Park

Álice and Tómmy are with their móther.
They are wálking in the párk.
The chíldren are tíred.
Their móther is tíred, tóo.

5   TOMMY: Cán we sít on the gráss, múm?
    MOTHER: Nó, you cán't, Tómmy.
             The gráss is wét.
    ALICE: Lóok, múm!
             Í can sée a bénch near that trée.

10   TOMMY: Wé can sít thére.
    MOTHER: Nó, you cán't, chíldren.
             The bénch is wét, tóo.
    ALICE: It's nót raíning, múm.
             The bénch ísn't wét.

15   MOTHER: Cán you sée a nótice on the bénch, Álice?
    ALICE: Yés, I cán.
    MOTHER: Whát does the nótice sáy?
    ALICE: I cán't réad it.
             Can yóu réad the nótice, Tómmy?

20   TOMMY: Í can réad it.
             It sáys 'Wét Páint'!

Answer these questions

A.   1   Are Tommy and Alice in the park?
     2   Are they with their mother?
     3   Are the children with their father?
     4   Are the children tired?
     5   Is their mother tired too?
     6   Can they sit on the grass?
     7   Is the grass wet?
     8   Can the children sit on the bench?
     9   Is the bench wet?
   10   Is it raining?
   11   Can they see a notice on the bench?
   12   Can Alice read the notice?
   13   Can Tommy read it?
   14   Does the notice say 'Wet Paint'?

B. 15 Are the children with their mother or with their father?
16 Are they walking or running?
17 Can the children see a bench or a pond? — *chasca*
18 Is the bench near a tree or near a pond?
19 Is the notice on the bench or on the grass?
20 Does the notice say 'Wet Paint' or 'Keep Off the Grass'?

C. 21 What are the children's names?
22 What are the children doing?
23 What can Alice see?
24 What is on the bench?
25 What does the notice say?

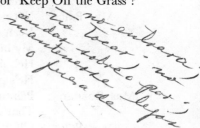

D. Mixed questions (Recorded)

E. Ask these questions
   Ask me
1a if the children's names are Alice and Tommy.
 b what their names are.
2a if they are walking in the park.
 b what they are doing.
3a if Alice can see a bench.
 b what Alice can see.
4a if the children can sit on the bench.
 b what the children can do.
5a if their mother can see a notice on the bench.
 b what their mother can see.
6a if the children can see the notice too.
 b what they can see.
7a if the notice says 'Wet Paint'.
 b what the notice says.

13

3 He's not an Artist

Mrs Róbinson is in her gárden.
She is stánding near the fénce.
She is tálking to her néighbour.
Her néighbour's náme is Mŕs Príce.

5 MRS ROBINSON: Good mórning, Mrs Príce.
Can I bórrow your ládder, pléase?

MRS PRICE: Nót nów, Mrs Róbinson.
I can gíve it to you this áfternóon.
My húsband is úsing the ládder nów.

10 He's úpstáirs.
He's páinting.

MRS ROBINSON: Páinting!
Thát's a níce hóbby!

MRS PRICE: Oh, it's nót his hóbby, Mrs Róbinson.

15 He dóesn't líke it.

MRS ROBINSON: Ís your húsband páinting a pícture?

MRS PRICE: Nó, he cán't páint píctures.
He ísn't an ártist.

MRS ROBINSON: Whát is he dóing?

20 MRS PRICE: He's páinting the báthroom!

Answer these questions
A. 1 Is Mrs Robinson in her garden?
2 Is she in her kitchen?
3 Is Mrs Robinson standing near the fence?
4 Is Mrs Robinson talking to Mrs Price?
5 Is Mrs Robinson talking to her husband?
6 Does Mrs Robinson want Mrs Price's ladder?
7 Can Mrs Robinson borrow Mrs Price's ladder now?
8 Can she borrow Mrs Price's ladder this afternoon?
9 Is Mr Price using the ladder now?
10 Is Mr Price upstairs?
11 Is he painting?
12 Is this his hobby?
13 Is Mr Price an artist?
14 Can he paint pictures?
15 Is Mr Price painting the bathroom?

B. 16 Is Mrs Robinson in the kitchen or in the garden?
17 Is Mrs Robinson talking to Mrs Price or to her husband?
18 Does Mrs Robinson want a ladder or a book?
19 Can she borrow the ladder this morning or this afternoon?
20 Is Mr Price upstairs, or is he in the garden?
21 Is he painting a picture, or is he painting the bathroom?

C. 22 What are Mrs Robinson and Mrs Price doing?
23 What does Mrs Robinson want?
24 What is Mr Price doing?

D. Mixed questions (Recorded)

E. Ask these questions
Ask me
1a if Mrs Robinson and Mrs Price are standing near the fence?
b what they are doing.
2a if Mrs Robinson wants a ladder.
b what Mrs Robinson wants.
3a if Mrs Price can give the ladder to Mrs Robinson.
b what Mrs Price can do.
4a if Mr Price is using the ladder.
b what he is using.
5a if Mr Price is painting a picture.
b what he is painting.
6a if he likes it.
b what he likes.
7a if this is his hobby.
b what his hobby is.
8a if he is an artist.
b what he is.

4 What is the Baby Doing?

NARRATOR: Jóhn Wílkins is in the líving-room.
His wífe, Máry, is in the kítchen.
She is cálling him.
MRS WILKINS: Ís the báby with yóu, Jóhn?
5 He's nót in the kítchen.
MR WILKINS: He ísn't hére, Máry.
He's úpstáirs.
MRS WILKINS: Pléase gó and sée, Jóhn.
He's véry quíet.
10 MR WILKINS: Áll ríght, Máry.
NARRATOR: Nów Mr Wílkins is úpstáirs.
MR WILKINS: He's nót in his róom, Máry.
MRS WILKINS: Ís he in óur róom?
MR WILKINS: Nó, he's nót.
15 Hé's in the báthroom.
MRS WILKINS: Whát's he dóing?
MR WILKINS: He's cléaning his shóes with your tóothbrush!

Answer these questions

A. 1 Is John in the living-room?
2 Is he in the kitchen?
3 Is John's wife in the kitchen?
4 Is her name Mary?
5 Is Mary calling him?
6 Is the baby with John?
7 Is the baby in the kitchen?
8 Is the baby upstairs?
9 Is the baby making a noise?
10 Is the baby quiet?
11 Is the baby in the bedroom?
12 Is he in the bathroom?
13 Is the baby cleaning his shoes?
14 Is he using Mary's toothbrush?

B. 15 Is John in the living-room or in the kitchen?
16 Is his wife in the living-room or in the kitchen?

17 Is his wife's name Mary or June?
18 Is the baby upstairs or downstairs?
19 Is the baby in the bedroom or in the bathroom?
20 Is the baby cleaning his shoes or his teeth?

C. 21 What is the name of John's wife?
22 What is John going to do?
23 What is the baby cleaning?
24 What is he using?

D. Mixed questions (Recorded)

E. Ask these questions
    Ask me
1a if Mary is calling her husband.
 b what she is doing.
2a if John can go upstairs.
 b what John can do.
3a if John is going to look in the bathroom.
 b what he is going to do.
4a if the baby is cleaning his shoes.
 b what he is cleaning.
5a if the baby is using a toothbrush.
 b what he is using.

5   In a Department Store

Mŕs Jénkins is in a depártment stóre.
She is góing to búy a cóat.
She is stánding near the cóunter.
She is wáiting for the shóp-assístant.

5   A fát lády is stánding near the cóunter, tóo.
She is lóoking at Mŕs Jénkins.
Nów she is tálking to Mŕs Jénkins.

FAT LADY: Excúse mé.
MRS JENKINS: Yés?

10   FAT LADY: Are you góing to sérve me?
I wánt a cóat.

MRS JENKINS: I'm sórry.
Í can't sérve you.

FAT LADY: Of cóurse you can sérve me.

15   Thát's yóur jób.

MRS JENKINS: It's nót my jób.
Í want a cóat, tóo.
Í'm a cústomer.
I'm nót a shóp-assístant!

Answer these questions

A.   1   Is Mrs Jenkins in a department store?
     2   Is she going to buy a coat?
     3   Is she going to buy a toothbrush?
     4   Is Mrs Jenkins standing near the counter?
     5   Is she waiting for the shop-assistant?
     6   Can she see a lady near the counter?
     7   Is the lady fat?
     8   Are Mrs Jenkins and the fat lady waiting for the shop-assistant?
     9   Is Mrs Jenkins going to serve the fat lady?
   10   Does the fat lady want a coat?
   11   Does she want a toothbrush?
   12   Can Mrs Jenkins serve the fat lady?
   13   Does Mrs Jenkins want a coat too?
   14   Is Mrs Jenkins a shop-assistant?
   15   Is Mrs Jenkins a customer?

B. 16 Is Mrs Jenkins going to buy a coat or a toothbrush?
17 Is she standing near the counter or near the door?
18 Is a lady standing near the counter or near the door?
19 Is the lady fat or thin?
20 Does the fat lady want a coat or a pair of shoes?
21 Is Mrs Jenkins a customer or a shop-assistant?

C. 22 What is Mrs Jenkins going to buy?
23 What is the fat lady doing?
24 What do Mrs Jenkins and the fat lady want?
25 What is Mrs Jenkins?

D. Mixed questions (Recorded)

E. Ask these questions
   Ask me
   1a if Mrs Jenkins is going to buy a coat.
    b what she is going to buy.
   2a if a fat lady is talking to Mrs Jenkins.
    b what the fat lady is saying.
   3a if Mrs Jenkins can serve the fat lady.
    b what Mrs Jenkins can do.
   4a if the fat lady wants a coat.
    b what the fat lady wants.
   5a if Mrs Jenkins is a shop-assistant.
    b what Mrs Jenkins is.
   6a if this is Mrs Jenkins' job.
    b what Mrs Jenkins' job is.
   7a if Mrs Jenkins and the fat lady are going to buy coats.
    b what they are going to buy.

6 A Modern Picture

Sálly Jónes is fíve yéars óld.
She góes to schóol évery dáy.
She páints píctures and bríngs them hóme.
Sálly shóws the píctures to her móther.
5   Her móther cán't understánd them.
MOTHER: Whát is thát, Sálly?
SALLY: It's a hóuse.
MOTHER: And whát are thése?
SALLY: Thése are róoms.
10   Thís róom is the kítchen.
Thát is my bédroom.
MOTHER: Whát are thóse gréen línes?
SALLY: They're nót línes, múm.
They're trées.
15   Thís trée is in the ský.
MOTHER: Ís thís an áeroplane?
SALLY: It's nót an áeroplane, múm.
It's yóu.
Yóu're in the ský, tóo.

Answer these questions

A. 1 Is Sally five years old?
2 Is she ten years old?
3 Does she go to school every day?
4 Does Sally paint pictures at school?
5 Does Sally leave the pictures at school?
6 Does she bring them home?
7 Does she show the pictures to her mother?
8 Can her mother understand them?
9 Can Sally understand her pictures?
10 Can mother see a house in Sally's picture?
11 Can she see lines in the picture?
12 Are the lines trees?
13 Is the tree in the sky?
14 Is Sally's mother in the picture too?

B. 15 Is Sally five or six?

20

16 Does she go to school or does she stay at home?
17 Does she paint pictures at school, or does she read books?
18 Does Sally bring the pictures home, or does she leave them at school?
19 Is Sally's mother looking at a picture or at a book?
20 Are the lines in the picture green or red?
21 Is the tree in the sky or near the house?

C. 22 What does Sally do at school?
23 What does she do with the pictures?
24 What does she show her mother?
25 What can her mother see in the picture?
26 What colour are the trees in Sally's picture?

D. Mixed questions (Recorded)

E. Ask these questions
   Ask me
   1a   if Sally goes to school every day.
    b   what she does every day.
   2a   if she paints pictures.
    b   what she paints.
   3a   if she brings the pictures home.
    b   what she brings home.
   4a   if she shows the pictures to her mother.
    b   what she shows to her mother.
   5a   if her mother can see a tree in the picture.
    b   what her mother can see.
   6a   if the tree is green.
    b   what colour it is.
   7a   if it is an aeroplane.
    b   what it is.

7 You Can't Park Here

Mŕ Máson is stánding in frónt of a cár.
He is lóoking at it.
It is a béautiful cár and it is véry bíg.
Mŕ Máson líkes bíg cárs.
5 A políceman is stánding behínd Mr Máson.
Hé is lóoking at the cár, tóo.
He is wríting in a nótebook.
Nów he is gíving a píece of páper to Mŕ Máson.

POLICEMAN: Excúse me, sír.
10 MR MASON: Yés?
POLICEMAN: Thís is for yóu.
MR MASON: Whát ís it?
POLICEMAN: It's a tícket.
MR MASON: A tícket?
15 POLICEMAN: Cán you sée that nótice?
MR MASON: Yés.
POLICEMAN: It says 'Nó Párking'.
You cán't párk your cár hére.
MR MASON: This ísn't my cár!

Answer these questions
A. 1 Is Mr Mason standing in front of a car?
    2 Is he in the car?
    3 Is he looking at the car?
    4 Is it a big car?
    5 Does Mr Mason like big cars?
    6 Can the policeman see Mr Mason?
    7 Is the policeman writing in a notebook?
    8 Is the policeman giving a piece of paper to Mr Mason?
    9 Is the piece of paper a ticket?
    10 Can Mr Mason see the notice?
    11 Does the notice say 'No Parking'?
    12 Does the notice say 'Parking'?
    13 Is this the policeman's car?
    14 Is it Mr Mason's car?

B. 15 Is Mr Mason looking at a car or at a van?
   16 Is it a big car or a small car?
   17 Does Mr Mason like big cars or small cars?
   18 Is the policeman standing behind Mr Mason, or is he in the car?
   19 Is he giving Mr Mason a ticket or a notebook?
   20 Does the notice say 'No Parking' or 'Parking'?

C. 21 What is Mr Mason doing?
   22 What does Mr Mason like?
   23 What is the policeman giving to Mr Mason?
   24 What does the notice say?

D. Mixed questions (Recorded)

E. Ask these Questions
   Ask me
   1a   if Mr Mason is standing in front of a car.
    b   what he is doing.
   2a   if Mr Mason likes big cars.
    b   what he likes.
   3a   if the policeman is writing in a notebook.
    b   what he is writing.
   4a   if he is going to give a ticket to Mr Mason.
    b   what he is going to give to Mr Mason.
   5a   if Mr Mason can see a notice.
    b   what he can see.
   6a   if the notice says 'No Parking'.
    b   what the notice says.

8 Next-door Neighbours

Mŕ Táylor is on a shíp.
He is góing to América.
He is tálking to a stránger.

MR TAYLOR: Dó you líve in Lóndon?
5 STRANGER: Yés, I dó.
I líve in Hámpstead.
MR TAYLOR: Hámpstead!
Í live in Hámpstead, tóo.
Lóndon's a fúnny pláce.
10 I dón't knów my néxt-dóor néighbour.
STRANGER: Í live in Pónd Stréet.
MR TAYLOR: Thát's fúnny!
Í live in Pónd Stréet, tóo.
STRANGER: Í live at númber 24 Pónd Stréet.
15 MR TAYLOR: Í live at númber 23!
Yóu're my néxt-dóor néighbour!
Mý name's Táylor.
STRANGER: Mý name's Bénnet.
TOGETHER: Hów do you dó?

Answer these questions
A. 1 Is Mr Taylor in his car?
2 Is he on a ship?
3 Is the ship going to America?
4 Is Mr Taylor talking to a stranger?
5 Does the stranger live in London?
6 Does Mr Taylor live in London too?
7 Do Mr Taylor and the stranger live in Hampstead?
8 Does Mr Taylor know his next-door neighbour?
9 Does Mr Taylor live in Pond Street?
10 Does the stranger live in Lake Street?
11 Does the stranger live in Pond Street too?
12 Are they next-door neighbours?
13 Is the stranger's name Taylor?
14 Is the stranger's name Bennet?

24

B. 15 Is Mr Taylor on a ship or in an aeroplane?
16 Is the ship going to America or Australia?
17 Is Mr Taylor talking to a friend or to a stranger?
18 Does the stranger live in London or in New York?
19 Do Mr Taylor and the stranger live in Pond Street or Lake Street?
20 Is the stranger's name Taylor or Bennet?

C. 21 What is Mr Taylor's address?
22 What is the stranger's address?
23 What is the stranger's name?

D. Mixed questions (Recorded)

E. Ask these questions
Ask me
1a if Mr Taylor is talking to a stranger.
 b what he is doing.
2a if Mr Taylor's address is 23 Pond Street, Hampstead.
 b what his address is.
3a if the stranger's name is Bennet.
 b what the stranger's name is.

Chapter 2
TO THE TEACHER

Summary of Question Forms

New forms which can be used in this chapter are given in italics.

A. Yes and No Tag Answers

Am/is/are	Do/does/*did*
Can	*Have/has*
Was/were	*Must*
Shall/will	

Negative questions by inversion using these auxiliaries

B. Questions with 'who'

C. Double questions joined by 'or'

D. Other question words

What	*Where*
Which	*Why*
When	*Whose*

E. Mixed questions (Recorded)

F. Asking questions

PARTICULAR DIFFICULTIES

Telling the time

The use of *any* in questions and negative answers.

Differentiating between 'Are they . . .?' and 'Are there . . .?'

9 Early One Morning

On Súndays/fáther tákes us for a dríve/into the cóuntry.//
We enjóy this véry múch.//
Lást Súnday/we gót up véry éarly.//
We sát in the cár/and wáited for fáther.//
5 At síx-thírty/móther and fáther were réady.//
Fáther sát behínd the whéel/and stárted the éngine.//
The cár dídn't móve.//
'Thát's fúnny,'/fáther sáid.//'It was áll ríght yésterday.'//
He tríed agáin,/but the cár dídn't móve.//
10 'There ísn't any pétrol in the tánk!'/my bróther Jímmy sáid.//
'You're ríght, Jímmy!'/fáther ánswered.//
'I'll gó and gét some pétrol from the gárage,'/Jímmy sáid.//
'It's hálf pást síx,'/my móther sáid.//'The gárage is shút.'//
'Whát shall we dó?'/I ásked.//
15 'We can gó back to béd/and gét up at níne o'clóck,'/fáther sáid.//
Móther and fáther wént back to béd,/but Jímmy and Í/stáyed in the cár.//
'Wé're not góing to sléep,'/we sáid.//
Súddenly,/fáther knócked at the wíndow of the cár.//
20 'Wáke up, chíldren,'/he sáid.//'It's níne o'clóck.'//

Answer these questions

A. 1 Did they get up very early last Sunday?
2 Did father start the car?
3 Did the car move?
4 Isn't there any petrol in the tank?
5 Can Jimmy go to the garage?
6 Is the garage shut?
7 Will father and mother stay in the car?
8 Won't the children stay in the car?
9 Did the children go to sleep?

B. 10 Who takes the children for a drive on Sundays?
11 Who started the engine?
12 Who will go back to bed?
13 Who woke up the children at nine o'clock?

28

C. 14 Do they go to the country on Sundays, or do they stay at home?

15 Did they get up early or late last Sunday?

16 Were mother and father ready at 6.30 or at 10.0 o'clock?

17 Did father start the engine, or did Jimmy start it?

18 Is there any petrol in the tank, or is the tank empty?

19 Will Jimmy get some petrol, or will he stay in the car?

20 Is the garage open or shut?

21 Did mother and father go back to bed, or did they stay in the car?

22 Did father wake up the children, or did mother wake up the children?

D. 23 When does father take the children to the country?

24 At what time were mother and father ready?

25 Whose car was it?

26 Where did father sit?

27 Why did mother and father go back to bed?

28 What did the children do?

29 When did father knock at the window of the car?

E. Mixed questions (Recorded)

F. Ask these questions

Ask me

1a if they go for a drive on Sundays.

b when they go for a drive.

2a if they got up early last Sunday.

b why they got up early last Sunday.

3a if mother and father were ready at six-thirty.

b what time mother and father were ready.

4a if the garage is open.

b why the garage isn't open.

5a if father woke up the children.

b when father woke up the children.

10 At the Hotel

'We wánt a róom on the fírst flóor,'/I sáid.//
'Cértainly, sír,'/the hótel mánager ánswered.//
'Háve you a róom/with a prívate báthroom?'/I ásked.//
'Yés, sír,'/the hótel mánager sáid.//'Hére are the kéys to númber
5 twénty-óne.'//
I tóok the kéys/and my wífe and Í wént úpstáirs.//
We unlócked the dóor of númber twénty-óne/and wént into the róom.//
We shút the dóor/and pút our cáses on the flóor.//
'Lísten!'/my wífe sáid.//There's a mán in this róom.//He's sínging.//
10 'You're ríght!'/I sáid.//'He's ín the báthroom!'//
I knócked at the dóor/of the báthroom.//The sínging stópped.//
'Whó is it?'/a vóice sáid.//
'Thís is óur róom,'/I ánswered.//'Whát are you dóing here?'//
'Yóur róom!'/the vóice ánswered ángrily.//'Thís is *mý* róom.//Pléase
15 gó awáy.//I'm táking a báth.'//
'I'll cáll the mánager,'/my wífe sáid.//
Júst thén/the dóor ópened/and the mánager cáme ín.//
'I'm véry sórry,'/he sáid.//'I máde a mistáke.//Yóur róom is néxt
dóor.//Hére are the kéys to númber twénty-twó.'//

Answer these questions

A. 1 Do you want a room on the first floor?
2 Is there a room with a private bathroom?
3 Did the manager give you the keys?
4 Didn't you go upstairs?
5 Did you go into room twenty-one?
6 Is there a man in the bathroom?
7 Will your wife call the manager?
8 Wasn't the manager sorry?
9 Didn't the manager make a mistake?
10 Is your room next door?
11 Did the manager give you the keys to number twenty-two?

B. 12 Who wants a room on the first floor?
13 Who gave you the keys?
14 Who is in the bathroom?
15 Who will call the manager?

16 Who has given you the keys to room twenty-two?

C. 17 Do you want a room on the first floor or on the ground floor?
18 Did the manager give you the keys to room twenty-one or room twenty-two?
19 Did you and your wife go upstairs, or did you stay downstairs?
20 Is the stranger in the bathroom or in the bedroom?
21 Is this your room, or is it the stranger's room?
22 Will your wife call the manager, or will you call him?
23 Did the manager come upstairs, or did your wife go downstairs?

D. 24 Which keys did the manager give you?
25 Where did you and your wife go?
26 Whose room was this?
27 What is the stranger doing in the bathroom?
28 Why was the man angry with you?
29 Why is the hotel manager sorry?

E. Mixed questions (Recorded)

F. Ask these questions
Ask me
1a if I want a room on the first floor.
b why I want a room on the first floor.
2a if the manager gave me the keys to room twenty-one.
b what the manager gave me.
3a if this is my room.
b whose room this is.
4a if my wife will call the manager.
b who she will call.
5a if the manager came upstairs.
b when the manager came upstairs.
6a if my room is next door.
b where my room is.

11 What's for Dinner?

'Whát's for dínner?'/Tím ásked.//
'I'm góing to frý some físh,'/Pát ánswered.//
'I dón't wánt any físh,'/Tím sáid.//'I had físh for lúnch.//We can gó
to a réstaurant this évening.'//
5 'Thát's a góod idéa,'/Pát ánswered.//
Tím and Pát wént to a réstaurant.//They sát at a táble/and a wáiter
bróught them a ménu.//
'I wánt some róast béef,'/Tím sáid.//'Whát do yóu want, Pát?'//
'I wánt a véal chóp,'/Pát sáid.//
10 Tím túrned to the wáiter.//
'Óne róast béef/and a véal chóp, pléase.//And we wánt some potátoes
and péas,'/he sáid.//
'I'm sórry, sír,'/the wáiter sáid.//'We háven't any róast béef/and we
háven't any véal chóps.'//
15 'But they're ón the ménu!'/Tím sáid ángrily.//
'I'm sórry, sír,'/the wáiter ánswered.//'That's yésterday's ménu.//
'Whát do you suggést?'/Tím ásked.//
'Wéll, sír,'/the wáiter sáid.//'We have some níce frésh físh.'//

Answer these questions
A.   1 Is Pat going to fry some fish?
    2 Does Tim want any fish?
    3 Will Tim and Pat go to a restaurant this evening?
    4 Did the waiter bring them a menu?
    5 Doesn't Tim want roast beef?
    6 Does Pat want a veal chop?
    7 Do they want any potatoes and peas?
    8 Can the waiter bring them roast beef and veal chops?
    9 Aren't they on the menu?
   10 Is this today's menu?
   11 Isn't it yesterday's?
   12 Can the waiter bring some fish?

B. 13 Who is going to fry some fish?
   14 Who went to the restaurant?
   15 Who brought the menu?

16 Who wants some roast beef?

17 Who ordered a veal chop?

C. 18 Is Pat going to fry some fish, or is she going to fry some veal chops?

19 Will Tim and Pat go to a restaurant, or will they stay at home?

20 Does Tim want roast beef, or does he want a veal chop?

21 Did Pat order some roast beef or a veal chop?

22 Did the waiter give them yesterday's menu or today's menu?

D. 23 What is Pat going to fry?

24 Why doesn't Tim want any fish?

25 Where did Tim and Pat go?

26 What did they order?

27 Why is the waiter sorry?

28 What can the waiter bring them?

E. Mixed questions (Recorded)

F. Ask these questions

Ask me

1a if Tim wants any fish.

 b why he doesn't want any fish.

2a if they can go to a restaurant.

 b where they can go.

3a if the waiter brought them a menu.

 b what the waiter brought them.

4a if Tim wants roast beef.

 b what Tim wants.

5a if they have any roast beef.

 b what they have.

6a if this is yesterday's menu.

 b which menu this is.

12   A Clever Cat

It was twó o'clóck in the mórning/and it was véry dárk.//
Mŕ Thómpson wóke up his wífe.//
'Iréne,'/he cálled sóftly,/'the báby's crýing.'//
Mŕs Thómpson sát up in béd and lístened.//
5   'Thát's not the báby, Jím,'/ she sáid.//'It's a cát!'//
'It cán't be,'/her húsband sáid.//'I'll gó and lóok.'//
Mŕ Thómpson gót up/and wént to the wíndow.//
'You're ríght, Iréne,'/he sáid.//'There's a cát in the gárden.// Lísten
to it!'//
10   'You múst stóp it, Jím,'/Mrs Thómpson sáid.//'Thát cát will wáke up
the báby.'//
'Whát can I dó?'/Mr Thómpson ásked.//'It's véry cóld.//I'm nót
going into the gárden.'//
'Thrów a shóe at it,'/his wífe suggésted.//
15   'I cán't do thát,'/Mr Thómpson ánswered.//
'Whý nót?'/his wífe ásked.//'Cán't you sée it?'//
'I can sée it véry wéll,'/Mr Thómpson sáid.//'But I cán't thrów a shóe
at it.//It's sítting on my gréenhouse!'//

Answer these questions

A.   1   Was it two o'clock in the afternoon?
2   Wasn't it two o'clock in the morning?
3   Didn't Mr Thompson wake up his wife?
4   Is the baby crying?
5   Can they hear a cat?
6   Won't Mr Thompson go and look?
7   Did he go to the window?
8   Can he see a cat in the garden?
9   Won't the cat wake up the baby?
10   Will Mr Thompson go into the garden?
11   Can't he throw a shoe at the cat?
12   Isn't the cat sitting on his greenhouse?

B.   13   Who woke up at two o'clock?
14   Who woke up Mrs Thompson?
15   Who can see a cat in the garden?

34

C. 16 Did Mr Thompson wake up at two o'clock or at four o'clock?
    17 Was his wife asleep or awake?
    18 Will Mr Thompson get out of bed, or will Mrs Thompson get out of bed?
    19 Did Mr Thompson go to the window, or did he go into the garden?
    20 Is the cat in the garden or on the roof?
    21 Is the cat on the greenhouse or in the greenhouse?

D. 22 What time was it?
    23 Why has Mr Thompson woken up his wife?
    24 What can they hear?
    25 Where did Mr Thompson go?
    26 Where was the cat?
    27 What must Mr Thompson do?
    28 Why won't Mr Thompson go into the garden?
    29 Where is the cat sitting?
    30 Why can't Mr Thompson throw a shoe at it?

E. Mixed questions (Recorded)

F. Ask these questions
    Ask me
    1a if it was two o'clock.
     b what time it was.
    2a if Mr Thompson woke up his wife.
     b when Mr Thompson woke up his wife.
    3a if Mr Thompson will look out of the window.
     b what he will do.
    4a if Mr Thompson got up.
     b when he got up.
    5a if he can see a cat.
     b what he can see.
    6a if he must stop it.
     b what he must do.

13 The Daily News

Mr Gréen wént to the néwsagent's/and bóught his mórning néws-paper.//
'Góod morning, Jóe,'/Mŕ Gréen sáid.//
'Good mórning, Mŕ Gréen,'/Jóe ánswered.//'The *Dáily News?*'//
5 'Yés, pléase,'/Mŕ Gréen sáid.//'Ís there any néws todáy?'//
'Nó,/there ísn't any néws todáy,'/Jóe ánswered.//'There was anóther múrder yésterday.//Some thíeves róbbed a bánk.//And some wórkmen wént on stríke at a fáctory.'//
'Ís that áll, Jóe?'/Mŕ Gréen ásked.//
10 'Thát's áll, Mŕ Gréen.//The sáme thíngs háppen évery dáy.//Ónly the námes and addrésses chánge.'//
'Wíll it ráin tomórrow, Jóe?'/Mŕ Gréen ásked.//
'Yés,/it wíll, Mŕ Gréen,'/Jóe ánswered.//'The páper sáys "Ráin tomórrow".'//
15 'The wéather dóesn't chánge,'/Mŕ Gréen sáid.//
'You're ríght, Mŕ Gréen,'/Jóe ánswered.//'Ráin yésterday,/ ráin todáy,/and ráin tomórrow.'//
Mŕ Gréen pícked up his néwspaper/and lóoked at it.//'Whý do we réad néwspapers, Jóe?'/he ásked.//
20 'It pásses the tíme,'/Jóe ánswered,/'and it kéeps me in búsiness.'//

Answer these questions

A. 1 Didn't Mr Green go to the newsagent's?
2 Did he buy a newspaper?
3 Did he buy any cigarettes?
4 Is there any news today?
5 Was there another murder yesterday?
6 Didn't some workmen go on strike?
7 Don't the same things happen every day?
8 Will it rain tomorrow?
9 Will the weather change?
10 Didn't it rain yesterday?

B. 11 Who went to the newsagent's?
12 Who sells newspapers?
13 Who wants the *Daily News*?

14 Who robbed a bank?
15 Who went on strike?

C. 16 Did Mr Green go to the newsagent's or to the chemist's?
17 Did he buy a newspaper or some cigarettes?
18 Does Mr Green read the *Daily News* or the *Daily Tribune?*
19 Was there a murder yesterday or the day before yesterday?
20 Does Mr Green sell newspapers or does Joe sell them?

D. 21 Where did Mr Green go?
22 What did he buy?
23 What is the name of the newspaper?
24 When did the workmen go on strike?
25 What does the newspaper say about the weather?
26 Why do we read newspapers?

E. Mixed questions (Recorded)

F. Ask these questions
    Ask me
1a if Mr Green went to the newsagent's.
 b why Mr Green went to the newsagent's.
2a if he bought a newspaper.
 b which newspaper he bought.
3a if he reads the *Daily News.*
 b which newspaper he reads.
4a if there is any news today.
 b why there isn't any news today.
5a if the workmen went on strike.
 b when the workmen went on strike.
6a if the weather will change.
 b when the weather will change.
7a if Joe is a newsagent.
 b what Joe is.

14 At the Grocer's

Mŕs Fórd lóoked at her shópping líst.//
'I wánt some bútter/and some chéese,'/she sáid,/'and a pácket of bíscuits.'//
'Is that áll, Mŕs Fórd?'/the grócer ásked.//
5   Mŕs Fórd lóoked at her líst agáin.//'Nó./I wánt some súgar,/some flóur/and a pácket of téa.'//
'Súgar,/flóur,/and téa,'/the grócer sáid/and pút them on the cóunter.//
'And a tín of tomáto sóup,'/Mŕs Fórd sáid.//
'We háven't any tomáto sóup,'/the grócer sáid.//
10   'Whát are thóse tíns/on that shélf?'/Mŕs Fórd ásked.
'Thése, Mŕs Fórd?'/the grócer ásked.//'They're tíns of tomátoes.//
Do you wánt a tín?'//
'Nó, thánk you.'//
'Is that áll, Mŕs Fórd?'//
15   'Yés, thánk you.//Pléase sénd them to my hóuse.//Óh,/and I wánt a dózen éggs, tóo,/but dón't sénd them.//Í'll cárry them.'//
'We can sénd the éggs, tóo,'/the grócer sáid.//
'Nó, thánk you,'/Mŕs Fórd sáid./'Your néw delívery bóy is véry cáreless.//Lást wéek/he drópped the éggs on my dóorstep.'//

Answer these questions

A. 1 Did Mrs Ford look at her shopping list?
    2 Does Mrs Ford want any butter?
    3 Doesn't she want any cheese?
    4 Did the grocer put the sugar on the counter?
    5 Doesn't Mrs Ford want a tin of tomato soup?
    6 Has the grocer any tomato soup?
    7 Are there any tins on the shelf?
    8 Do these tins contain tomato soup?
    9 Don't they contain tomatoes?
   10 Will the grocer send the things to Mrs Ford's house?
   11 Can he send the eggs too?
   12 Will he send the eggs?

B. 13 Who looked at the shopping list?
   14 Who wants some butter and cheese?

15 Who will send the things to Mrs Ford's house?

16 Who will carry the eggs?

17 Who is very careless?

C. 18 Did Mrs Ford look at the shopping list, or did the grocer look at it?

19 Does Mrs Ford want some biscuits or some bread?

20 Does she want a tin of tomato soup or a tin of tomatoes?

21 Are the tins on the shelf or on the counter?

22 Will the grocer send the things, or will Mrs Ford carry them?

23 Will Mrs Ford take the eggs with her, or will the grocer send them?

D. 24 Where was Mrs Ford?

25 What did the grocer put on the counter?

26 What did Mrs Ford see on the shelf?

27 What did the tins contain?

28 Where will the grocer send the things?

29 Why will Mrs Ford carry the eggs?

E. Mixed questions (Recorded)

F. Ask these questions

Ask me

1a if Mrs Ford is at the grocer's.

b where Mrs Ford is.

2a if she wants any butter.

b what she wants.

3a if there are any tins on the shelf.

b where the tins are.

4a if they contain tomato soup.

b what they contain.

5a if the grocer will send the things.

b when he will send them.

15 Late for Work

I gót hóme at síx o'clóck in the évening.//My wífe ópened the frónt
dóor for me.//
'Good évening, Téd,'/she sáid.//
'Good évening, my déar,'/I ánswered.//
5 'Are you tíred?'/she ásked.//
'Nó,'/I ánswered,/'I'm nót tíred,/but I'm véry húngry.'//
'Dínner will be réady in hálf an hóur,'/she sáid.//
I tóok off my cóat/and sát dówn.//My wífe sát besíde me.//
'Díd you cátch your tráin this mórning?'/she ásked.//
10 'Nó,'/I ánswered,/'I míssed it.//I rán áll the wáy to the státion/and
gót there/at fóur mínutes pást níne.'//
'Whích tráin did you cátch?'//
'The 9.15.'//
'Whát tíme did you gét to the óffice?'/she ásked.//
15 'At tén o'clóck,'/I ánswered.//
'At tén o'clóck!'/my wífe excláimed.//'Wásn't the bóss ángry?'//
'Nó,/he wásn't at the óffice.'/I sáid.//'He arríved at tén-thírty.//
Hé missed hís train, tóo!'//

Answer these questions

A. 1 Did you get home at six o'clock?
2 Didn't your wife open the door for you?
3 Are you tired?
4 Aren't you hungry?
5 Won't dinner be ready in half an hour?
6 Did you catch your train this morning?
7 Didn't you miss the train?
8 Didn't you get to your office at ten o'clock?
9 Wasn't the boss angry?
10 Was the boss at the office?
11 Did the boss arrive at 10.30?
12 Didn't he miss his train too?

B. 13 Who got home at six o'clock?
14 Who opened the door for you?
15 Who is hungry?

40

16 Who caught the 9.15 train this morning?
17 Who arrived at the office at 10.30?

C. 18 Did you get home at six o'clock or at seven o'clock?
19 Did your wife open the front door or the back door?
20 Were you tired or hungry?
21 Will dinner be ready in half an hour or in an hour?
22 Did you miss your train this morning, or did you catch it?
23 Did you get the eight o'clock train or the 9.15?
24 Did you get to the office at ten o'clock or at twelve?
25 Did your boss get to the office before you or after you?

D. 26 What time did you get home?
27 When will dinner be ready?
28 Which train did you catch this morning?
29 What time did you get to the office?
30 Why wasn't the boss angry?
31 When did the boss arrive at the office?

E. Mixed questions (Recorded)

F. Ask these questions
   Ask me
   1a   if I got home at six o'clock.
    b   what time I got home.
   2a   if I'm tired.
    b   why I'm tired.
   3a   if dinner will be ready in half an hour.
    b   when dinner will be ready.
   4a   if I missed the train this morning.
    b   why I missed the train this morning.
   5a   if I caught the 9.15.
    b   which train I caught.
   6a   if the boss was angry.
    b   why he wasn't angry.

16 Help!

I am stáying at the Róyal Hotél.//
This mórning/I wálked past a róom on the fírst flóor.//
Súddenly,/I héard a wóman's vóice.//
'Hélp!'/the wóman shóuted.
5 Thén I héard a mán's vóice.//
'Dón't móve or I'll shóot you!'/the mán shóuted ángrily.
'Pléase dón't shóot me,'/the wóman críed.//
The mán láughed.//Thén I héard a shót!//
I knócked at the dóor lóudly.//
10 'Cóme ín,'/the wóman sáid sóftly.//
I rúshed into the róom.//
'Whát's the mátter?'/I ásked the wóman.//'Cán I hélp you?'//
'Whó áre you?'/the wóman ásked ángrily.//
'I héard a shót,'/I sáid.//'Áre you áll ríght?'//
15 The wóman láughed.//'Of cóurse I'm áll ríght.'
She túrned to the mán.//
'Pút your gún in your pócket,'/she sáid.//
'Whát's háppening?'/I ásked.//
'We're nót quárrelling,'/the mán sáid.//'We are áctors.// We are
20 léarning our párts.'//

Answer these questions

A. 1 Aren't you staying at the Royal Hotel?
2 Were you on the first floor this morning?
3 Didn't a woman call for help?
4 Did you hear a shot?
5 Didn't you go into the room?
6 Was the woman dead?
7 Was she all right?
8 Didn't the man have a gun?
9 Did he put the gun in his pocket?
10 Are the man and the woman quarrelling?
11 Are they actors?
12 Aren't they learning their parts?

B. 13 Who is staying at the Royal Hotel?
14 Who heard a shot this morning?

15 Who went into the room?

16 Who has a gun?

17 Who put the gun in his pocket?

C. 18 Are you staying at the Royal Hotel or at the Grand Hotel?

19 Did a woman call for help, or did a man call for help?

20 Did you go into the room, or did you call the manager?

21 Was the woman alive or dead?

22 Did the man put the gun in his pocket, or did he put it on the shelf?

23 Are the man and the woman quarrelling or acting?

D. 24 Which is your hotel?

25 When did you hear a shout?

26 Why did you go into the room?

27 Where did the man put his gun?

28 What are the man and the woman doing?

E. Mixed questions (Recorded)

F. Ask these questions

Ask me

1a if I am staying at the Royal Hotel.

 b where I am staying.

2a if I heard a shout.

 b what I heard.

3a if the man will shoot the woman.

 b why he will shoot her.

4a if I went into the room.

 b where I went.

5a if the man put his gun in his pocket.

 b where the man put his gun.

6a if they are actors.

 b what they are.

Chapter 3
TO THE TEACHER

Summary of Question Forms

New forms which can be used in this chapter are given in italics.

A. Yes and No Tag Answers

Am/is/are	Do/does/did
Can/*could*	Was/were
Have/has	Shall/will/*would*
Must	*May*
Ought	

Negative questions by inversion using these auxiliaries
Question tags

B. Questions with 'who'

C. Double questions joined by 'or'

D. Other question words
What
Where
Which
Why
When
Whose
How

E. Mixed questions (Recorded)

F. Asking questions

PARTICULAR DIFFICULTIES
How much/old/big, etc.
Do/does/did with *have* (in the sense of experience, take, receive, etc.): e.g. Did you have a good time?
Do/does/did with causative *have*: Did you have your hair cut?
Questions involving *say, hope, think, know*, etc. where no tense-change and only an obvious pronoun change is required.
Also: *sorry, glad, sense*, etc. . . . *(that)*.

17 A Pair of Glasses

Lást wéek/I had my éyes tésted.//
'Mý wìfe thínks I néed glásses,'/I expláined to the optícian.//
'I knów I dón't need glásses.//I can sée véry wéll.'//
The optícian tésted my éyes.//'You óught to wéar glásses, sir,'/he
5   sáid.//'Cóme and chóose a páir of fràmes.'//
'I can sée véry wéll withóut glásses,'/I insísted,/'but if yóu say I
néed them,/I'll háve to háve them.'//
The optícian did not ánswer me.//He shówed me some fràmes.//
'Chóose a páir of thése,'/he sáid.//'Thése fràmes are made of plástic,/
10 and thése are made of métal.//Thése are tórtoise-shéll and are ráther
déar.'//
'I'll have the plástic ónes,'/I sáid.//
'Dó you thínk they súit you?'/he ásked/and hánded me a mírror.//
I réached out for the mírror/and míssed.//It cráshed to the flóor/and
15 bróke into a thóusand pìeces.//
'I'm véry sórry,'/I sáid and blúshed.//
'It dóesn't mátter,'/the optícian ánswered./'We lóse a lót of mírrors
like thát.'//
'Wéll,'/I sáid,/'I cértainly néed glásses.'//
20 'You cértainly dó,'/the optícian ánswered with a smíle.//'Your wìfe
was ríght.'//

Answer these questions

A. 1 Did you have your eyes tested last week?
    2 Your wife thinks you need glasses, doesn't she?
    3 Do you think you need glasses?
    4 Ought you to wear glasses?
    5 Tortoise-shell frames are rather dear, aren't they?
    6 Will you buy tortoise shell frames?
    7 Will you buy plastic frames?
    8 You broke a mirror, didn't you?
    9 Were you sorry?
   10 You can't see very well, can you?
   11 Was your wife right?

B. 12 Who thinks you need glasses?
   13 Who tested your eyes?

14 Who broke the mirror?
15 Who often loses mirrors?
16 Who was right?

C. 17 Did you have your eyes tested, or did your wife have her eyes tested?
18 Did you go to an optician or to a doctor?
19 Will you buy a pair of plastic frames or a pair of metal ones?
20 Did you drop the mirror, or did the optician drop it?
21 Did you break the mirror, or did you break a pair of glasses?
22 Were you sorry or pleased?
23 Was your wife right or wrong?

D. 24 When did you have your eyes tested?
25 What does your wife think?
26 What did the optician show you?
27 What kind of frames did you choose?
28 Why didn't you choose tortoise-shell frames?
29 How did you break the mirror?
30 Whose mirror was it?

E. Mixed questions (Recorded)

F. Ask these questions
   Ask me
   1a if I had my eyes tested.
    b why I had my eyes tested.
   2a if my wife thinks I need a pair of glasses.
    b what my wife thinks.
   3a if I went to an optician.
    b where I went.
   4a if I will buy plastic frames.
    b what kind of frames I will buy.
   5a if I broke the optician's mirror.
    b how I broke the optician's mirror.

18 Our New Secretary

The télephone ráng/and our néw sécretary,/Míss Símpson,/ánswered it.//
'Máy I spéak to Mŕ Cálder, pléase?'/a vóice sáid.//
'Whó is spéaking pléase?'/Míss Símpson ásked.//
5 'Mŕ Álan Bríght,'/the vóice sáid.//
Míss Símpson put her hánd over the móuthpíece/and spóke to Mŕ Cálder.//
'It's Mŕ Álan Bríght, sir,'/she sáid.//'He wánts to spéak to you.'//
10 'Whát,/agáin!'/Mŕ Cálder excláimed.//'He wánts to séll us thóse néw týpewriters, dóesn't he?'//
'Yés, sir,'/Míss Símpson sáid.//'He cálled yésterday.'//
'And he ráng up fíve tímes lást wéek.//We dón't néed néw týpewriters.//I tóld him thát yésterday,'/Mŕ Cálder sáid.
15 'Whát shall I sáy, sir?'/Míss Símpson ásked.//
'Sáy that I'm nót in my óffice,'/Mŕ Cálder sáid cróssly.//
Míss Símpson spóke into the recéiver.//'Mŕ Bríght,'/she sáid,/'I'm afráid you cán't spéak to Mŕ Cálder nów.//Mŕ Cálder sáys that he's nót in his óffice.'//

Answer these questions
A. 1 The telephone rang, didn't it?
2 Didn't Miss Simpson answer it?
3 Was it Mr Bright?
4 Does Mr Bright want to speak to Mr Calder?
5 Does Mr Calder want to speak to Mr Bright?
6 Mr Bright wants to sell Mr Calder some typewriters, doesn't he?
7 Did Mr Bright call yesterday?
8 Does Mr Calder need any new typewriters?
9 Is Mr Calder in his office?
10 Will Mr Calder speak to Mr Bright?
11 Will he speak to his secretary?

B. 12 Who answered the telephone?
13 Who is speaking?
14 Who wants to speak to Mr Calder?

15 Who rang five times last week?
16 Who will tell Mr Bright that Mr Calder is not in his office?

C. 17 Did Miss Simpson answer the telephone, or did Mr Calder answer it?
18 Does Mr Bright want to speak to Mr Calder, or does he want to speak to Miss Simpson?
19 Does Mr Bright want to sell some typewriters or some tape-recorders?
20 Is Mr Calder in his office, or has he gone out?

D. 21 What's the name of the new secretary?
22 Whose secretary is she?
23 What does Mr Bright want to sell to Mr Calder?
24 How many times did Mr Bright telephone last week?
25 Why doesn't Mr Calder want any new typewriters?
26 What will Miss Simpson say to Mr Bright?

E. Mixed questions (Recorded)

F. Ask these questions
   Ask me
   1a   if the telephone rang.
    b   when the telephone rang.
   2a   if Miss Simpson answered the telephone.
    b   when Miss Simpson answered the telephone.
   3a   if Mr Bright wants to speak to Mr Calder.
    b   why he wants to speak to Mr Calder.
   4a   if Mr Bright wants to sell some typewriters.
    b   what he wants to sell.
   5a   if Mr Calder wants to buy any new typewriters.
    b   why he doesn't want to buy any new typewriters.
   6a   if Mr Calder is in his office.
    b   where Mr Calder is.
   7a   if Mr Bright rang up last week.
    b   how many times Mr Bright rang up last week.

19 Two Tramps and a Dog

Twó trámps were wálking alóng a quíet róad.//A sórry-looking dóg was fóllowing them.//
'We've had a bád dáy,/Jóe,'/the fírst trámp sáid.//'We háven't any móney/and we cán't get ánything to éat.'//
5 'We'll find sómething,'/the sécond trámp ánswered chéerfully.// Súddenly,/the trámps sáw a cár in the dístance.//It was cóming towárds them véry quíckly.//Bóth the trámps móved to óne síde,/but the dóg stáyed in the míddle of the róad.//
The dríver tríed to stóp the cár,/but it was tóo láte.//The cár hít
10 the dóg/and kílled it.//The dríver gót óut of the cár/and wént towárds the fírst trámp.//
'Póor little dóg,'/the trámp sáid sádly.//
'I'm térribly sórry,'/the dríver sáid.//'I tríed to avóid your dóg/but I cóuldn't.'//He tóok out his wállet/and gáve fíve póunds to the
15 trámp.//'Will thát be áll ríght?'/the dríver ásked.//
'Yés, sir,/thánk you, sir,'/the trámp sáid.//
The dríver gót ínto his cár/and dróve awáy.//
'Póor little dóg,'/the fírst trámp sáid/and pút the móney into his pócket.//
20 'Whóse dóg wás it?'/the sécond trámp ásked.//

Answer these questions
  A. 1 Was a dog following the two tramps?
     2 Have the tramps any money?
     3 Can't they get anything to eat?
     4 The tramps saw a car, didn't they?
     5 The car was coming towards them, wasn't it?
     6 Did the tramps stay in the middle of the road?
     7 Did the dog stay in the middle of the road?
     8 Didn't the car run over the dog?
     9 The driver was very sorry, wasn't he?
    10 Didn't he give the tramps some money?
    11 The tramps accepted the money, didn't they?
    12 Did the dog belong to the tramps?

  B. 13 Who was walking along the road?

14 Who saw the car?
15 Who killed the dog?
16 Who was very sorry?
17 Who has given the tramps some money?

C. 18 Were the tramps walking along a road or across a field?
  19 Did they see a car or a lorry? _caminar - correr fuerte_
  20 Did the tramps stay in the middle of the road, or did they
     move to one side? _atropellar - posar en -_
  21 Did the car run over a dog or a cat? _aire de ; hojea_
  22 Did the first tramp accept the money, or did he refuse it?
  23 Did the driver stay with the tramps, or did he drive away? _reparar_

D. 24 Where were the tramps?
  25 Why can't the tramps get anything to eat?
  26 Why did the tramps move to one side of the road?
  27 Why did the driver try to stop the car?
  28 How much did the driver give the tramps?
  29 What did the driver do after this?

E. Mixed questions (Recorded)

F. Ask these questions
  Ask me
  1a if a dog was following the tramps.
   b why the dog was following the tramps.
  2a if the tramps could get anything to eat.
   b why they couldn't get anything to eat.
  3a if they could see a car in the distance.
   b what they could see.
  4a if the car stopped near the tramps.
   b where the car stopped.
  5a if the driver gave the tramps £5.
   b how much the driver gave the tramps.

20 The Horse Couldn't Sing

'Díd you enjóy the ópera lást níght?'/Fréd ásked.//
'Véry múch,'/I ánswered.//
'Í must gó, tóo,'/Fréd sáid.//'Wás it a góod perfórmance?'//
'I dón't knów,'/I ánswered.//
5 'But you sáw it, dídn't yóu?'//
'Wéll,/I ónly saw hálf of it.'//
'Díd you léave befóre the énd of the perfórmance?'/Fréd ásked.//
'Yés and nó,'/I ánswered.//
'Whát do you méan/"yés and nó"?'/Fréd ásked.//
10 'Wéll,'/I sáid,/'éveryone léft befóre the énd.'//
'Then you *dídn't* enjóy it,'/Fréd sáid.//
'Nó,/I enjóyed it véry múch,'/I ánswered.//
'Then whý did éveryone léave befóre the énd?'//
I láughed and sáid,/'It was véry fúnny réally./There were twó líve
15 hórses in the ópera.//The síngers léd them cárefully acróss the stáge
a féw tímes.//But in the sécond áct,/óne of the hórses júmped off
the stáge/and rán róund the théatre.//It refúsed to gó báck.//Then
the cúrtain cáme dówn/and we áll hád to léave.'//
'Perháps the hórse cóuldn't síng,'/Fréd suggésted.//

Answer these questions

A. 1 Did you go to the opera last night?
2 Does Fred want to go to the opera too?
3 Didn't Fred ask you if you enjoyed the performance?
4 Did you see the whole opera?
5 You left before the end of the performance, didn't you?
6 Were you the only person who left before the end of the performance?
7 Were there two live horses in the opera?
8 Did one of the horses jump off the stage?
9 It ran round the theatre, didn't it?
10 Did you all have to leave the theatre?
11 You couldn't stay at the theatre, could you?

B. 13 Who went to the opera last night?
14 Who wants to go to the opera too?

15 Who left the theatre before the end of the performance?
16 Who led the horses across the stage?

C. 17 Did you go to the opera or to a concert?
18 Did you see the whole opera, or did you only see half of it?
19 Did a horse jump off the stage in the first act or in the second act?
20 Did the horse run around the theatre, or did it go back on the stage?
21 Did the performance come to an end, or did it continue?

D. 22 When did you go to the opera?
23 How much of the opera did you see?
24 How many horses were taking part in the opera?
25 What did one of the horses do?
26 In which act did this happen?
27 Why did you all have to leave?

E. Mixed questions (Recorded)

F. Ask these questions
   Ask me
   1a   if I went to the opera last night.
   b   where I went last night.
   2a   if I saw the whole opera.
   b   why I didn't see the whole opera.
   3a   if everyone left before the end of the performance.
   b   when everyone left.
   4a   if there were two live horses in the opera.
   b   how many horses there were.
   5a   if one of the horses jumped off the stage.
   b   what one of the horses did.
   6a   if I had to leave.
   b   why I had to leave.

21 Easy to Drive

A crówd of péople were stánding in the stréet.//They were lóoking at a néw cár.//The cár was óutsíde a shówróom.//It was a néw módel/ and mány péople wánted to sée it.//A sálesman nóticed the crówd/and cáme into the stréet.//

5   'It's a béautiful módel, ísn't it?'/the sálesman sáid.
'It cértainly ís,'/a mán agréed.//'Ís it automátic?'//
'Óh yés,'/the sálesman ánswered próudly.//'There aren't ány géars in thís cár.//You préss your fóot down/and dríve awáy.// It's véry éasy to dríve.//Éven a wóman can dríve it without ány dífficulty.'//

10   'I dídn't líke that remárk,'/a wóman sáid.//
'I'm sórry, mádam,'/the sálesman ánswered.//'I dídn't nótice you.// Ányway,/I was ónly jóking.'//
'Gíve us a demonstrátion,'/the wóman sáid.//'Dríve a féw yárds.'//

15   The sálesman smíled with pléasure.//He gót into the cár/and stárted the éngine.//Then he préssed a bútton/and the cár súddenly wént báckwards.//There was a lóud crásh/and the cár went thróugh the wíndow of the shówróom.//

Answer these questions
A. 1 Were there any people in the street?
   2 Weren't they looking at a new car?
   3 Was it an old model?
   4 Didn't the salesman come into the street?
   5 It's an automatic car, isn't it?
   6 Has it any gears?
   7 It's not difficult to drive an automatic car, is it?
   8 Won't the salesman give the crowd a demonstration?
   9 He'll drive a few yards, won't he?
   10 Did the salesman get into the car?
   11 Did the car move forward?
   12 Didn't the car move backwards?
   13 There was a loud crash, wasn't there?
   14 The salesman broke the showroom window, didn't he?

B. 15 Who noticed the crowd in the street?
   16 Who can drive an automatic car without difficulty?
   17 Who objected to the salesman's remark about women drivers?

54

18 Who will give a demonstration?
19 Who broke the showroom window?

C. 20 Were the people in the street looking at a new car or at an old one?
21 Has the car any gears, or is it automatic?
22 Is it easy or difficult to drive?
23 Does the salesman think that women are good drivers or bad drivers?
24 Did the salesman give a demonstration, or did a member of the crowd give a demonstration?
25 Did the car go forward, or did it reverse?

D. 26 Where were the people standing?
27 Why did the salesman come into the street?
28 Why is this car easy to drive?
29 Which car did the salesman drive?
30 How did the salesman break the showroom window?

E. Mixed questions (Recorded)

F. Ask these questions
Ask me
1a   if the car was outside the showroom.
 b   where the car was.
2a   if the salesman noticed the crowd.
 b   what the salesman noticed.
3a   if the car is easy to drive.
 b   why it is easy to drive.
4a   if the salesman will give a demonstration.
 b   when the salesman will give a demonstration.
5a   if the salesman drove a few yards.
 b   how far he drove.
6a   if the salesman broke the showroom window.
 b   how the salesman broke the showroom window.

22 It's Never Too Late

Tómmy's bírthday is on Márch í3th.//Two wéeks agó,/Tómmy wróte a létter to his áunt Lúcy.//His móther cáme into his róom/while he was wríting his létter.//

'Whát are you dóing, Tómmy?'/she ásked.//

5   'I'm wríting a létter to áunt Lúcy,'/Tómmy ánswered.//

Tómmy's móther was véry surprísed/because Tómmy néver wrítes létters to ányone.//

'Áre you invíting her to your bírthday párty?'/his móther ásked.//

'Nó,/I'm nót,'/Tómmy ánswered.//'Áunt Lúcy néver cómes to my
10   bírthday párties.'//

'Whát have you wrítten?'/his móther ásked.//'Wíll you réad me the létter?'//

'Áll ríght.'/Tómmy sáid.//'But I've ónly wrítten two línes.// I'll réad them to you.//Lísten.//"Dear Áunt Lúcy,// Thánk you véry
15   múch for your bírthday présent.//I hópe . . ." '//

His móther interrúpted him,/'But Tómmy,/Áunt Lúcy hásn't sént you a bírthday présent yét.'//

'I knów,'/Tómmy replíed.//'I'm nót thánking her for thís yéar's présent.//I'm thánking her for lást yéar's!'//

Answer these questions

  A. 1 Is Tommy's birthday on March 13th?
      2 Didn't Tommy write a letter to his aunt two weeks ago?
      3 His mother was very surprised, wasn't she?
      4 Tommy never writes letters, does he?
      5 Will Tommy invite his aunt to his birthday party?
      6 Does Aunt Lucy ever come to Tommy's parties?
      7 Didn't Tommy read part of the letter to his mother?
      8 Has Tommy written two lines of the letter?
      9 Is Tommy thanking his aunt for her birthday present?
    10 Has she sent a birthday present this year?
    11 Did she send a present last year?
    12 Did Tommy write to his aunt last year to thank her for her present?

  B. 13 Who is writing a letter?
    14 Who came into the room when Tommy was writing?

15 Who was surprised at Tommy?
16 Who has written two lines of the letter?
17 Who sent Tommy a present last year?

C. 18 Is Tommy's birthday on March 13th or on May 13th?
19 Will Tommy write a letter to his aunt or his uncle?
20 Does Tommy often write letters or does he seldom write letters?
21 Is Tommy thanking his aunt for this year's present or for last year's?

D. 22 Whose birthday is on March 13th?
23 When did Tommy write a letter to his aunt?
24 Why is Tommy's mother surprised?
25 Why hasn't Tommy invited his aunt to his birthday party?
26 When did Tommy's aunt send him a birthday present?

E. Mixed questions (Recorded)

F. Ask these questions
Ask me
1a if Tommy wrote a letter to his aunt two weeks ago.
 b how long ago Tommy wrote a letter to his aunt.
2a if his mother came into the room.
 b when his mother came into the room.
3a if Tommy's mother was surprised.
 b why she was surprised.
4a if Tommy ever writes letters.
 b why he never writes letters.
5a if he has written two lines.
 b how much he has written.
6a if Tommy will read the letter to his mother.
 b what Tommy will do.
7a if his aunt sent him a present last year.
 b when his aunt sent him a present.

23　The Amateur Photographer

I wént into our lócal chémist's shóp/and hánded a róll of film to Mŕ
Dódd.//'I wánt to háve thís film devéloped and prínted please,'/I
sáid.//'Whén will it be réady?'//
　　'On Túesday,'/Mŕ Dódd ánswered.//
5　'I hópe they're succéssful thís tíme,'/I sáid/and léft the shóp.//
I retúrned the fóllowing Túesday.//'Ís my fílm réady?'/I ásked.//
Mŕ Dódd lóoked at me sádly.//'Hére it is, Mŕ Méad,'/he sáid.//
I ópened the énvelope éagerly/and lóoked at the phótographs.//
'There are ónly éight phótographs hére!'/I excláimed.//'I óught to
10　have thírty-síx!'//
　　'Díd you táke the phótographs yoursélf?'/Mŕ Dódd ásked.//
I nódded.//
　　'I'm afráid you spóilt the róll of fílm,'/he sáid.//'Your cámera léts
in líght.'//
15　I lóoked at the éight phótographs.//Twó of them were álmost bláck/
and thrée of them were álmost whíte.//I láughed when I sáw the rést
of them.//'My síster has no légs in thís one.// And lóok at this trée!//
It's grówing out of my bróther's héad!'//
　　'I'm afráid they're nót véry succéssful,'/Mŕ Dódd sáid.//
20　'I'll néver be a photógrapher!'/I sáid sádly.//

Answer these questions
A.　1　Did Mr Mead go to the chemist's?
　　2　Does Mr Mead want to have a film developed and printed?
　　3　Will it be ready on Tuesday?
　　4　Mr Mead went back to the chemist's the following Tuesday,
　　　　didn't he?
　　5　The film was ready, wasn't it?
　　6　Were there only eight photographs?
　　7　Mr Mead took the photographs himself, didn't he?
　　8　Is he a good photographer?
　　9　Were the eight pictures successful?
　　10　Didn't Mr Mead spoil the roll of film?
　　11　Did Mr Mead laugh at the photographs?
　　12　The photographs weren't very good, were they?

B. 13 Who went to the chemist's?
14 Who wants to have the film developed and printed?
15 Who will collect the photographs on Tuesday?
16 Who took the photographs?

C. 17 Did Mr Mead go to the chemist's or to the grocer's?
18 Will the film be ready on Tuesday or on Thursday?
19 Did Mr Mead get eight photographs or thirty-six?
20 Is Mr Mead's camera in good condition, or does it let in light?
21 Were the photographs successful or unsuccessful?

D. 22 Where did Mr Mead take his roll of film?
23 What did Mr Mead want?
24 When will the film be ready?
25 How many photographs did Mr Mead get from Mr Dodd?
26 Why isn't Mr Mead's camera very good?
27 Why did Mr Mead laugh at the photograph of his sister?

E. Mixed questions (Recorded)

F. Ask these questions
Ask me
1a if Mr Mead will have the film developed and printed.
b where Mr Mead will have the film developed and printed.
2a if it will be ready on Tuesday.
b when it will be ready.
3a if the photographs were successful.
b why they weren't successful.
4a if he spoilt the film.
b how he spoilt the film.
5a if there are only eight photographs.
b how many photographs there are.
6a if Mr Mead will ever become a good photographer.
b why he will never become a good photographer.

59

24 It's Quicker on Foot

'Háve you préssed the bútton?'/Júdy ásked.//
   'Yés,'/Fránk ánswered.//'The líft is cóming.//Lóok,//it's at the fóurth flóor.'//Fránk póinted at the númbers over the dóor of the líft.//
   'It will néver cóme to the séventh flóor,'/Júdy sáid.//'Lóok,// it's
5 at the thírd flóor nów.//It's góing dówn agáin.//We have béen here for fíve mínutes.//We cán't wáit áll dáy.//Í'm going to wálk dówn the stáirs.'//
   'Wéll Í'm not going to wálk dówn áll thóse stáirs,'/Fránk sáid.//
   'I'll wáit for you on the gróund flóor,'/Júdy sáid.//
10   'I'll be thére befóre you,'/Fránk replíed.//
   Júdy wálked down the stáirs.//She díd not húrry.//Whén she réached the gróund flóor,/she lóoked for Fránk.//He wásn't thére.// She lóoked at the númbers over the dóor of the líft.//The líft was at the fóurth flóor.//The háll pórter was lóoking at the númbers, tóo/and
15 Júdy spóke to him.//
   'Whát has háppened to the líft?'/she ásked.//
   'It has stópped betwéen the thírd and fóurth flóors,'/the pórter ánswered.//'That's the thírd tíme this mórning!'//

Answer these questions

A. 1 Has Frank pressed the button?
     2 Is the lift coming?
     3 Are there any numbers over the door of the lift?
     4 Judy isn't going to wait for the lift, is she?
     5 She's going to walk down the stairs, isn't she?
     6 She's been there for five minutes, hasn't she?
     7 Will Frank walk down the stairs too?
     8 Won't Frank get to the ground floor before Judy?
     9 Did Judy hurry down the stairs?
     10 Frank wasn't on the ground floor, was he?
     11 Hasn't the lift stopped between the third and fourth floors?
     12 Isn't Frank in the lift?

B. 13 Who pressed the button?
     14 Who is going to walk down the stairs?
     15 Who is going to wait for the lift?

16 Who reached the ground floor first?

17 Who said, 'It has stopped between the third and fourth floors.'?

C. 18 Did Frank press the button, or did Judy press it?

19 Is Judy going to walk down the stairs, or is she going to wait for the lift?

20 Did Judy go down the stairs quickly or slowly?

21 Did she see Frank on the ground floor, or did she see the hall porter?

D. 22 Why is Judy going to walk downstairs?

23 Where will Judy wait for Frank?

24 What was the hall porter doing on the ground floor?

25 What did Judy ask the hall porter?

26 What has happened to the lift?

27 How many times has this happened this morning?

E. Mixed questions (Recorded)

F. Ask these questions

Ask me

1a if Frank has pressed the button.

b why he has pressed the button?

2a if the lift is at the third floor.

b where the lift is.

3a if Judy is going to walk down the stairs.

b why she is going to walk down the stairs.

4a if Judy hurried.

b why she didn't hurry.

5a if Frank was on the ground floor.

b where Frank was.

6a if the lift has stopped between floors.

how many times it has stopped between floors.

Chapter 4
TO THE TEACHER

Summary of Question Forms
New forms which can be used in this chapter are given in italics.

A. Yes and No Tag Answers
Am/is/are   Do/does/did
Can/could   Was/were
Have/has/*had*   Shall/will/*should*/would
Must   May
Ought
Negative questions by inversion using these auxiliaries
Question tags

B. Questions with 'who'

C. Double questions joined by 'or'

D. Other question words
What   Where
Which   Why
When   Whose
How

E. Mixed questions (Recorded)

F. Asking questions

G. Oral reproduction

PARTICULAR DIFFICULTIES
Questions involving the use of the passive. These have been confined to the following constructions: Simple Present; Simple Past; Future; Present Perfect; no agents; no hanging prepositions.
The use of 'else'.
Questions involving *say* and *tell* followed by a tense change.

25 First Flight

Fíve tóurists wálked slówly acróss the aírfield/where a véry smáll áircraft was wáiting for them.//The pláne was úsed on lócal flíghts/ and hád ónly twó éngines.//

The pássengers gót ínto the pláne/and sát dówn.//

5 'Fásten your séat-bélts pléase,'/the áir hóstess sáid.//

An óld lády túrned to the áir hóstess.//'Pléase hélp me with this bélt,'/she ásked,//'I have néver béen on an áeroplane befóre/and I féel ráther nérvous.'//

'Dón't wórry,'/the áir hóstess sáid kíndly.//'Thése plánes are the 10 sáfest in the wórld.'//

Thén the hóstess wént róund/with a tráy of swéets.//She óffered a swéet to éach of the pássengers.//

'Táke one of thése,'/she sáid to the óld lády.//'It will hélp you to swállow.'//

15 Súddenly,/the pláne begán to sháke and ráttle.//It móved quíckly down the rúnway/and slówly clímbed into the áir.// Whén the pláne was in the áir,/the hóstess wént to the óld lády agáin.//'Dídn't the swéet hélp you to swállow?'/she ásked.//

'Nó,/I'm afráid it dídn't,'/the óld lády ánswered.//'But it tóok my 20 mínd off the pláne.//Máy I háve anóther one pléase?'//

Answer these questions
A. 1 Was the plane used for local flights?
    2 It had only two engines, hadn't it?
    3 Did the passengers fasten their seat-belts?
    4 The old lady has never been on a plane before, has she?
    5 Doesn't she feel rather nervous?
    6 Didn't the hostess give some sweets to the passengers?
    7 Will the old lady accept a sweet?
    8 The plane took off, didn't it?
    9 Didn't the sweet help the old lady to swallow?
    10 Did the old lady want another sweet?

B. 11 Who told the passengers to fasten their seat-belts?
    12 Who feels nervous?
    13 Who has given the passengers some sweets?
    14 Who wants another sweet?

C. 15 Was the plane used for local flights or for international flights?

16 Did it have two engines or four engines?

17 Did the old lady feel nervous or calm?

18 Did the hostess offer the passengers sweets or chocolate?

19 Did the plane take off, or did it remain on the runway?

D. 20 How many tourists were going to travel by plane?

21 How many engines did the plane have?

22 What did the air hostess tell the passengers to do?

23 Why couldn't the old lady fasten her seat-belt?

24 What did the hostess give each passenger?

25 Why did the air hostess give sweets to the passengers?

26 How did the sweet help the old lady?

E. Mixed questions (Recorded)

F. Ask these questions

Ask me

1a if the passengers had to fasten their seat-belts.

b what the passengers had to do.

2a if the old lady needs help.

b why the old lady needs help.

3a if the old lady feels nervous.

b how she feels.

4a if the hostess gave the passengers some sweets.

b what the hostess gave the passengers.

5a if the plane took off.

b when the plane took off.

G. Oral reproduction

1 Conduct the dialogue between the old lady and the air hostess.

2 Describe what happened after the passengers boarded the plane.

26 Dinner for Two

Máx Róberts is a báchelor.//He líves in a smáll flát in Lóndon.//
Máx not only enjóys éating fóod,/he énjoys prepáring it as wéll.//
His fávourite hóbby is cóoking.//He has had só múch práctice,/that
he has becóme an éxpert cóok.//
5   His síster, Ánne, cálled on him lást Súnday évening.//It was néarly
dínner-tíme/and Máx was in the kítchen.//He was wéaring an ápron/
and prepáring a méal.//
'You wíll stáy to dínner, of cóurse,'/Máx sáid.//
'I'm stárving!'/Ánne sáid.//'Ís there enóugh fóod for bóth of us?'//
10   'I hópe so,'/Máx ánswered.//
Ánne lífted the líd of the sáucepan.//'Mḿ,'/she sáid.//'It smélls
delícious.//Whát ís it?'//
'It's a Méxican dísh,'/Máx sáid.//'Véry spécial.'//
'You'll be a góod wífe to sóme lúcky wóman,'/Ánne remárked.//
15   'I dón't knów about thát,'/Máx ánswered.//'But thís dísh óught to
be góod.//I've been prepáring it for fíve hóurs.'//
'Thére's enóugh fóod hére for tén péople!'/Ánne sáid/as she lóoked
into the sáucepan.//'Áre you expécting cómpany?'//
'Nó,'/Máx replíed,/'I was going to éat it áll mysélf.'//

Answer these questions
A. 1 Is Max married?
2 He's a bachelor, isn't he?
3 Max lives in a small flat, doesn't he?
4 Isn't Max a good cook?
5 Will Max's sister stay to dinner?
6 Is there enough food for both of them?
7 Max has prepared a Mexican dish, hasn't he?
8 Has Max been preparing the meal for several hours?
9 He isn't expecting company, is he?
10 He didn't intend to eat all that food himself, did he?

B. 11 Who is an expert cook?
12 Who called on Max last Sunday evening?
13 Who was preparing food at the time?
14 Who is going to stay to dinner?

C. 15 Is Max Roberts a bachelor, or is he married?
  16 Does he live in a small flat or in a large house?
  17 Was Max in the kitchen or in the dining-room when his sister called last Sunday?
  18 Was Max cooking or was he washing dishes?
  19 Was Max preparing a Spanish dish or a Mexican dish?

D. 20 Where does Max live?
  21 What is Max's favourite hobby?
  22 When did his sister call on him?
  23 Where was Max at the time?
  24 What was Max doing when his sister called?
  25 What sort of dish was Max preparing?
  26 How long has he been preparing his dinner?
  27 Why did his sister ask him if he was expecting company?

E. Mixed questions (Recorded)

F. Ask these questions
  Ask me
  1a   if Max lives in a small flat.
   b   where Max lives.
  2a   if cooking is his favourite hobby.
   b   what his favourite hobby is.
  3a   if Max was wearing an apron.
   b   what Max was wearing.
  4a   if he has been working in the kitchen for five hours.
   b   how long he has been working in the kitchen.
  5a   if there is enough food for ten people.
   b   how much food there is.

G. Oral reproduction
  1 Conduct the dialogue between Max and Anne.
  2 Describe what happened after Anne called on Max last Sunday.

27 The Student Teacher

My cóusin, Jóhn, is a univérsity stúdent.//Lást yéar/he wént to Ítaly/
and stáyed thére for twó mónths.//I was surprísed that Jóhn was áble
to háve/such a lóng hóliday/becáuse he néver has ány móney.//
    'Hów did you mánage it, Jóhn?'/I ásked.//'I thóught you were
5 góing to stáy for twó wéeks.'//
    'It was éasy,'/Jóhn ánswered.//'I gót a jób.'//
    'A jób!'/I excláimed.//'Whát did you dó?'//
    'I gáve Énglish léssons to a grócer,'/Jóhn ánswered.//'His náme is
Luígi.//We have becóme gréat fríends.'//
10   'But you're nót a téacher,'/I sáid.//
    'I tóld Luígi I cóuldn't téach,'/Jóhn expláined.//'But he insísted
on háving conversátion léssons.//He wánted to práctise his Énglish.//
He has a lót of Américan cústomers,/so it is impórtant for him to spéak
Énglish.//I spént thrée hóurs a dáy tálking to him.//In retúrn/he gáve
15 me a róom,/thrée méals a dáy/and a líttle pócket móney.'//
    'Díd your púpil léarn múch Énglish?'/I ásked.//
    'I dón't knów,'/Jóhn sáid,/'but Í léarnt a lót of Itálian!'//

Answer these questions
  A. 1 Is your cousin John still at school?
     2 He's a university student, isn't he?
     3 Didn't John go to Italy last year?
     4 He stayed there for two months, didn't he?
     5 Did John intend to stay in Italy for so long?
     6 He's always short of money, isn't he?
     7 Didn't he teach English in Italy?
     8 Was his pupil a butcher?
     9 His pupil was a grocer, wasn't he?
    10 Did Luigi want to practise his English?
    11 Luigi has a lot of American customers, hasn't he?
    12 Did John learn any Italian?

  B. 13 Who taught English in Italy last year?
    14 Who wanted to practice his English?
    15 Who has a lot of American customers?
    16 Who learnt a lot of Italian?

C. 17 Is John a university student, or is he still at school?

18 Is John rich, or is he always short of money?

19 Did John stay in Italy for two weeks or two months?

20 Did John get a job as a teacher or as a grocer?

21 Did John teach English or Italian?

22 Did Luigi want to practise speaking or writing?

D. 23 When did John go to Italy?

24 How long did he stay there?

25 Why were you surprised when you heard this?

26 How long did John originally intend to stay in Italy?

27 How did John manage to stay in Italy for two months?

28 What did John teach?

29 Why did Luigi want to practise his English?

30 What did John get in return for the lessons he gave?

E. Mixed questions (Recorded)

F. Ask these questions

Ask me

1a if John stayed in Italy for two months.

b how long he stayed there.

2a if John was going to stay in Italy for two weeks.

b how long he was going to stay there.

3a if John taught English.

b what John taught.

4a if Luigi wanted to practise his English.

b why Luigi wanted to practise his English.

5a if Luigi learnt any English.

b why he didn't learn any English.

G. Oral reproduction

1 Conduct the dialogue between John and his cousin.

2 Give an account of John's experiences in Italy.

28 The Bag They Missed

The pólice recéived a repórt/that síx mén had stópped a ván.//
The ván was cárrying fáctory wáges/and the mén had attácked the
dríver.//They had tíed him úp/and had stólen óne of the bágs.//
Áfter séarching for thrée hóurs/the pólice fóund the ván néar the
5 ríver.//The dríver was sítting on a bág/in the ván and his hánds
were tíed behínd his báck.//The thíeves had tíed a hándkerchief
róund his móuth/so that he wóuldn't shóut.//The pólice clímbed
into the báck of the ván/and fréed the dríver. Thén they ásked him
whát had háppened.//
10 'I was stópped sóon áfter I léft the bánk,'/the dríver expláined.//
'Síx mén stópped my ván/and máde me dríve to the ríver.//"Íf you
shóut,"/óne of them sáid,/"we'll shóot you."//Whén I gót to the
ríver,/they tíed me úp.//Thén they thréw me into the báck of the
ván.//There were twó bágs in the báck/and the thíeves tóok óne
15 of them.'//
'Hów much móney díd the bág contáin?'/a pólice ófficer ásked.//
'It dídn't contáin ány móney at áll,'/the dríver láughed.//'It
was fúll of létters.//Thís one contáins áll the móney.//I've been
sítting on it for thrée hóurs!'//

Answer these questions
  A. 1 Had six men stopped a van?
    2 Was the van carrying goods?
    3 It was carrying wages, wasn't it?
    4 Hadn't the thieves tied up the driver?
    5 The police found the van, didn't they?
    6 The thieves had attacked the driver, hadn't they?
    7 Could the driver shout for help?
    8 Weren't there two bags in the back of the van?
    9 Did the thieves take them both?
    10 Did the bag the thieves took contain any money?
    11 Has the driver been sitting in the back of the van for three
      hours?

  B. 12 Who stopped the van?
    13 Who had tied up the driver and stolen one of the bags?
    14 Who found the van?

C. 15 Was the van carrying wages or goods?

16 Was the van stopped by thieves or by the police?

17 Did the thieves tie up the driver, or did they shoot him?

18 Did the thieves leave the van near the river, or did they drive away in it?

19 Did the thieves take one of the bags or both of them?

20 Did the bag the thieves took contain money or letters?

D. 21 What was the van carrying?

22 How long did the police search for the van?

23 Why couldn't the driver shout for help?

24 Where did the thieves leave the van?

25 What would the thieves have done if the driver had shouted for help?

26 Which bag did the thieves take?

E. Mixed questions (Recorded)

F. Ask these questions

Ask me

1a if the van was carrying factory wages.

b what the van was carrying.

2a if the thieves had tied up the driver.

b why they had tied up the driver.

3a if the police found the van near the river.

b where the police found the van.

4a if the driver was stopped soon after he left the bank.

b when the driver was stopped.

5a if the driver shouted for help.

b why he didn't shout for help.

6a if the bag the thieves took contained any money.

b what the bag contained.

G. Oral reproduction

1 Describe what happened when the thieves stopped the van.

2 Put yourself in the driver's position. Give an account of what happened.

29 Ready Money

A yóung mán wént to a cár shówroom.//He was wéaring rúbber
bóots/and a dírty jácket.//He néeded a haírcut bádly/and was
únsháven.//The yóung mán exámined an expénsive cár cárefully/
and then túrned to spéak to the sálesman.//
5 'Hów múch does thís cár cóst?'/he ásked.//
'Óne thóusand twó húndred and eíghteen póunds,'/the sálesman
sáid.//
'I'll have síxtéen of them,'/the yóung mán sáid.//
The sálesman smíled.//He fóund it hárd to bé políte.//'You are
10 jóking, of cóurse,'/he sáid.//'I'm afráid we cán't hélp you.//Thís
cár is nót for sále.'//
The sálesman shówed his cústomer the dóor/and the yóung mán
léft the shóp withóut a wórd.//He wént to a shówroom on the óther
síde of the stréet/and ásked for síxtéen cárs.//The sécond sálesman
15 was políte and hélpful.//The yóung mán tóok a búndle of nótes out
of his pócket/and páid for the cárs in cásh.//He expláined that the
cárs were for himsélf/and his fífteen cólleagues.//He sáid that hé
and his cólleagues wórked on a Norwégian físhing-bóat.//'We have
áll éarned a lót of móney this séason,'/the mán sáid,/'and we wánt to
20 búy cárs.'//
Náturally,/the sécond sálesman was delíghted.//

Answer these questions

A. 1 Was the young man wearing rubber boots?
  2 He was wearing a dirty jacket too, wasn't he?
  3 Didn't he need a haircut and a shave?
  4 Did he ask the price of a car?
  5 It was an expensive one, wasn't it?
  6 Does the man want to buy sixteen cars?
  7 The salesman didn't believe him, did he?
  8 Will the young man buy the cars at another shop?
  9 Does he work on a fishing boat?
  10 Has he earned a lot of money this year?
  11 Have his colleagues earned a lot of money too?

B. 12 Who wanted to buy sixteen cars?
  13 Who thought the young man was joking?

14 Who works on a fishing-boat?
15 Who has earned a lot of money this year?

C. 16 Was the young man dressed in a suit, or was he wearing rubber boots and a dirty jacket?
17 Did he want to buy a cheap car or an expensive one?
18 Did he want one car or sixteen cars?
19 Was the first salesman helpful or unhelpful?
20 Did the young man go to another shop, or did he stay in the same shop?
21 Did he pay for the cars in cash or by cheque?

D. 22 Why did the first salesman think the young man was joking?
23 Where was the second car showroom?
24 How many cars did the man want to buy?
25 How did the man pay for the cars?
26 Where did the young man work?
27 Why did he want sixteen cars?

E. **Mixed questions** (Recorded)

F. **Ask these questions**
    Ask me
1a if the young man was wearing rubber boots.
 b what he was wearing.
2a if the car cost £1218.
 b how much the car cost.
3a if the man wanted sixteen cars.
 b how many cars the man wanted.
4a if the young man had a bundle of notes in his pocket.
 b what he had in his pocket.
5a if he and his friends want to buy cars.
 b what he and his friends want to buy.

G. **Oral reproduction**
 1 Conduct the dialogue between the young man and the two salesmen.
 2 Give an account of the young man's experiences with the two salesmen.

30 A Dirty Suit

'You múst have thís súit cléaned,'/Mŕs Fíeld sáid to her húsband.//
'It's véry dírty.'//She héld up a dárk súit for him to exámine.//
'Lóok!'//she sáid.//'There are stáins on the frónt/and dírty márks
róund the póckets of your tróusers.//Thís súit is só dírty,/it will stánd
5 úp by itsélf!'//
    'Áll ríght,/I'll táke it to the cléaner's,' Mŕ Fíeld ánswered.//
    'I cán't understánd/why you álways búy dárk súits,'/Mrs Fíeld
wént on.//'Whý don't you búy/a féw líght-cóloured súits for a chánge?
//Líght-cóloured súits are múch nícer.//They will máke you lóok
10 yóunger, tóo.'//
    'Perháps they wíll,'/Mŕ Fíeld sáid.//'But they will gét véry dírty
in Lóndon.//Lóndon áir ísn't exáctly cléan/and líght-cóloured súits
will shów all the dírt.//I'll háve to háve them cléaned ónce a mónth.'//
    'Thát's bétter than ónce a yéar,'/Mrs Fíeld replíed.//'Dárk súits
15 get júst as dírty,/but they dón't shów it.'//
    'Thát,'/Mŕ Fíeld sáid with a smíle,/'is whý I wéar them.'//

Answer these questions

A. 1 Was Mr Field's suit very clean?
       2 Were there any stains on it?
       3 There were dirty marks round the pockets too, weren't there?
       4 Will Mr Field take the suit to the cleaner's?
       5 Does Mr Field always buy dark suits?
       6 Doesn't his wife prefer light-coloured suits?
       7 Won't light-coloured suits show the dirt?
       8 Light-coloured suits have to be cleaned often, don't they?
       9 Do light-coloured suits show the dirt as much as dark ones?
      10 Mr Field prefers dark suits, doesn't he?

B. 11 Who told Mr Field to have his suit cleaned?
      12 Who likes light-coloured suits?
      13 Who prefers dark suits?
      14 Who has his suits cleaned once a year?

C. 15 Was Mr Field's suit clean or dirty?
      16 Does Mr Field always buy dark suits or light-coloured ones?
      17 Is the air in London clean or dirty?

74

18 Must a light-coloured suit be cleaned once a year or once a month?

19 Does Mr Field wear dark suits because he likes dark colours, or because dark suits don't show the dirt?

D. 20 What did Mrs Field show her husband?
21 Whose suit was it?
22 What did Mr Field agree to do with the suit?
23 Why does Mrs Field want her husband to buy light-coloured suits?
24 How often must a light-coloured suit be cleaned?
25 How often does Mr Field have his dark suits cleaned?
26 Why does Mr Field prefer dark suits?

E. Mixed Questions (Recorded)

F. Ask these questions
   Ask me
1a if he must have his suit cleaned.
 b why he must have his suit cleaned.
2a if Mr Field will take the suit to the cleaner's.
 b when he will take it to the cleaner's.
3a if he always buys dark suits.
 b why he always buys dark suits.
4a if he likes light-coloured suits.
 b why he doesn't like light-coloured suits.
5a if a light-coloured suit would get dirty in London.
 b why it would get dirty.
6a if he will have to have his suits cleaned once a month.
 b how often he will have to have his suits cleaned.
7a if dark suits show the dirt.
 b why they don't show the dirt.

G. Oral reproduction
1 Conduct the dialogue between Mr Field and his wife.
2 Give an account of Mrs Field's views about men's suits and Mr Field's views about them.

31   A Day's Shooting

Mý úncle is a kéen spórtsman.//He óften góes shóoting during the wéek-énd/and úsually comes hóme/with a bág fúll of bírds.// Lást Súnday évening/he cáme hóme éarlier than úsual.//He dídn't sáy ánything when he cáme ín.//He thréw his bág on the táble/and
5 sát by the fíre.//He lóoked tíred and cróss.//

'Dídn't you háve a góod dáy, déar?'/his wífe ásked.//

'Whát do yóu thínk?'/he ánswered cróssly/and póinted at the bág.//

'Lóok at this bág!//There's ónly óne bírd in it/and it cóst me a lót of móney!'//

10 'Wéren't there ány bírds?'/my áunt ásked kíndly.//

'Húndreds of them!'/my úncle sáid,/'but Í spent the dáy/árguing with a fármer.'//

'Whát háppened, déar?'/she ásked.//

'I shót my fírst bírd/at fíve o'clóck this mórning.// Sóon áfterwards/
15 I áimed at anóther one/and fíred.//But I dón't knów whát háppened. //I thínk I slípped/because I dídn't shóot the bírd.//I hít aców and kílled it.//The fármer who ówned it got véry annóyed with me.//I árgued with him for hóurs/and ín the énd/I hád to páy him £50!'//

Answer these questions

A. 1 Does your uncle often go shooting?
2 Did he go shooting last Sunday?
3 He came home early, didn't he?
4 Was his bag empty?
5 Had he spent the day shooting?
6 Had he spent a lot of money?
7 Was he angry?
8 Weren't there any birds?
9 There were plenty, weren't there?
10 Your uncle didn't kill a cow, did he?
11 Your uncle had to pay £50, didn't he?

B. 12 Who is a keen sportsman?
13 Who often goes shooting?
14 Who went shooting last Sunday?
15 Who killed a cow?
16 Who had to pay £50?

C. 17 Does your uncle like shooting or fishing?
  18 Did he have a bad day last Sunday, or did he have a good day?
  19 Did he shoot one bird or several?
  20 Did he shoot the cow by accident or on purpose?
  21 Was the farmer pleased or angry?
  22 Did your uncle have to pay the farmer £50 or £20?

D. 23 When does your uncle usually go shooting?
  24 Where did he throw his bag when he came in?
  25 Where did he sit?
  26 What was in his bag?
  27 How had your uncle spent the day?
  28 Why did he spend the day arguing with the farmer?
  29 How much did he have to pay?

E. Mixed questions (Recorded)

F. Ask these questions
  Ask me
  1a if my uncle goes shooting during the week-end.
   b when he goes shooting.
  2a if he shot many birds last Sunday.
   b why he didn't shoot many birds last Sunday.
  3a if he spent the day arguing with a farmer.
   b how he spent the day.
  4a if he killed a cow.
   b how he killed the cow.
  5a if he had to pay £50.
   b how much he had to pay.

G. Oral reproduction
  1 Conduct the dialogue between your uncle and aunt.
  2 Describe how your uncle spent last Sunday.

32 A Quiet Life

Whén Mr Fínch retíred,/he bóught a smáll cóttage/in a séaside víllage.//The cóttage was búilt in fífteen eíghty-eíght,/but was in véry góod condítion.//Mŕ Fínch was lóoking fórward to a quíet lífe,/ but in the súmmer hólidays/he gót a shóck.//Húndreds of tóurists/
5 cáme to the séaside víllage.//Mŕ Fínch's cóttage/was the móst ínteresting búilding in the víllage/and mány of the tóurists/cáme to sée it./ / From mórning till níght/there were tóurists óutside the cóttage.// They képt lóoking thróugh wíndows/and mány of them/éven wént ínto Mŕ Fínch's gárden.//Thís was tóo múch for Mŕ Fínch.//He
10 decíded to dríve the unwélcome vísitors awáy,/so he pút a nótice in the wíndow.//The nótice sáid://'If you wánt to sátisfy your curiósity, /cóme ín/and lóok róund.// Príce: // tén pénce.// Mŕ Fínch was súre that the vísitors would stóp cóming/ but he was wróng. //The númber of vísitors incréased/ and Mŕ Fínch spént évery
15 dáy/shówing them róund his cóttage.//'I cáme here to retíre,/nót to wórk as a guíde,'/he compláined.//Ín the énd,/he sóld the cóttage/and bóught a smáll, módern hóuse.//It is an uníteresting líttle pláce/and nó one wánts to sée it.//But it is cértainly quíet and péaceful!//

Answer these questions
A. 1 Had Mr Finch retired? yes
2 He had bought a small cottage in a seaside village, hadn't he?
3 Was the cottage built in 1588? yes
4 Was the cottage quiet and peaceful in the summer holidays?
5 Didn't the tourists want to see Mr Finch's cottage?
6 Mr Finch didn't like tourists, did he?
7 Could Mr Finch stop the visitors from coming?
8 Does Mr Finch want to work as a guide?
9 He sold his cottage, didn't he?
10 He's bought a modern house, hasn't he?

B. 11 Who retired to a seaside village?
12 Who wants a quiet life?
13 Who wanted to see Mr Finch's cottage?
14 Who has sold the cottage and bought a modern house?

C. 15 Had Mr Finch retired, or had he gone on holiday?

16 Did he buy an old cottage or a modern one?
17 Did a lot of tourists come to see Mr Finch's cottage, or did only a few come to see it?
18 Did Mr Finch put a notice in the window or on the door?
19 Did the number of tourists increase or decrease?
20 Did Mr Finch continue to live in his cottage, or did he sell it?
21 Has he bought another old cottage, or has he bought a modern house?

D. 22 When was Mr Finch's cottage built?
23 Why had Mr Finch bought it?
24 Where was the cottage?
25 Why didn't Mr Finch like living there?
26 How did Mr Finch try to stop the visitors from coming?
27 What did Mr Finch do with the cottage?
28 What did he buy?
29 Why is he pleased with his small modern house?

E. Mixed questions (Recorded)

F. Ask these questions
Ask me
1a if Mr Finch bought a small cottage.
 b what Mr Finch bought.
2a if it was built in 1588.
 b when it was built.
3a if he enjoyed living there.
 b why he didn't enjoy living there.
4a if he charged his visitors ten pence.
 b how much he charged his visitors.
5a if he had to leave the cottage.
 b why he had to leave the cottage.

G. Oral reproduction
Describe in detail what happened after Mr Finch bought a small cottage in a seaside village.

Chapter 5
TO THE TEACHER

Summary of Question Forms

New forms which can be used in this chapter are given in italics.

A. Yes and No Tag Answers

Am/is/are	Do/does/did
Can/could	Was/were
Have/has/had	Shall/will/should/would
Must	May/*Might*
Ought	

Negative questions by inversion using these auxiliaries
Question tags
Emphatic questions: You do like ice-cream, don't you?

B. Questions with 'who'

C. Double questions joined by 'or'

D. Other question words

What	Where
Which	Why
When	Whose
How	

Questions ending in prepositions

E. Mixed questions (Recorded)

F. Asking questions

G. Oral Reproduction and Free Expression

PARTICULAR DIFFICULTIES

Questions involving the use of the passive (all tenses).
Questions involving the use of *would rather* and *had better*.
Questions with *-ever* forms (whenever, wherever, etc.).

81

33 Money Problems

Mý bróther, Hénry, has an éxcellent jób at a bánk.//I cóuldn't belíeve him/when he tóld me/that he had decíded to gíve it úp.// Thóugh I tríed to máke him chánge his mínd,/I fáiled complétely.// 'You should réconsíder your decísion,'/I sáid.//'You have alréady
5 spént fíve yéars in the bánk/and you could háve a wónderful caréer.// You míght becóme a bánk mánager/by the tíme you're thírty-fíve.'// 'I knów,'/Hénry ánswered.//'I've got nó compláints with the bánk.// It's a pléasant jób/in pléasant surróundings/and we kéep cívilized
10 hóurs.//The bánk mánager tóld me that my próspects were éxcellent.'// 'Then whý do you wánt to léave?'/I excláimed.// *ceremias ; me dió)*
'It's the móney,'/Hénry sáid.//
'But you're gétting a góod sálary,'/I ánswered.//
'I dón't méan thát,'/Hénry sáid.//'Whát do I dó at the bánk?//
15 Wéll,/át the móment/áll I dó is to cóunt móney.//I fínd it véry depréssing.'//
'Whát's depréssing about cóunting móney?'/I ásked,/unáble to fóllow the lógic of Hénry's árgument.//
'You dón't understánd,'/Hénry ánswered.//'I enjóy cóunting my
20 ówn móney,/but I háte cóunting óther péople's!'//

Answer these questions

A. 1 Has your brother got a good job?
2 Didn't he tell you that he was going to give it up?
3 You could hardly believe it, could you?
4 You did try to make him change his mind, didn't you?
5 Should Henry reconsider his decision?
6 Did you succeed in making him change his mind?
7 Might Henry become a bank manager by the time he's thirty-five?
8 He's got excellent prospects, hasn't he?
9 He's getting a good salary, isn't he?
10 Does Henry like counting other people's money?

B. 11 Who's got a good job at a bank?
12 Who wants to give up his job?
13 Who might become a bank manager by the time he's thirty-five?

14 Who told Henry that his prospects were excellent?
15 Who has been trying to persuade Henry to keep his job?

C. 16 Does Henry work at a bank or at a factory?
17 Has Henry been working at the bank for five years or for ten years?
18 Does Henry work in pleasant surroundings or in unpleasant surroundings?

D. 19 Where does Henry work?
20 What has Henry decided to do?
21 Why should Henry reconsider his decision?
22 How long has Henry been working at the bank?
23 At what age might he become a bank manager?
24 Why has Henry got no complaints with the bank?
25 Why does Henry find his job depressing?

E. Mixed questions

F. Ask these questions
Ask me
1a if Henry works at a bank.
 b where Henry works.
2a if he has decided to give it up.
 b why he has decided to give it up.
3a if he should reconsider his decision.
 b why he should reconsider his decision.
4a if he might become a bank manager.
 b when he might become a bank manager.
5a if the bank manager told him that his prospects were good.
 b what the bank manager told him.

G. Oral reproduction and free expression
1 Conduct the dialogue between Henry and his brother.
2 Describe Henry's attitude to the bank and to his work.
3 Discuss the advantages and disadvantages of working at a bank.

34 A Spanish Holiday

Whén Álec retúrned to wórk lást Mónday,/Bób ásked him hów he had spént his hóliday.//

'You wént to Spáin, dídn't you?'/Bób ásked.//

'Thát's ríght,'/Álec ánswered.//'Thrée wéeks in the sún/and nów
5 I've got a yéar's wórk ahéad of me.//Stíll,/I múst sáy I enjóyed mysélf.//I wént swímming évery dáy/and I éven sáw a búllfight.'//

'Díd you?'/Bób sáid.//'Hów wás it?'//

'Véry fúnny, réally,'/Álec ánswered.//

'I've néver thóught of a búllfight as béing fúnny,'/Bób remárked.//
10 'Wéll, thís óne wás,'/Álec replíed.//'The búllfighter was a shów-man.//He arríved at the ríng in a hélicopter.//The hélicopter círcled round the ríng a féw tímes/and then the búllfighter lánded by pára-chute.//He lánded álmost in the míddle of the ríng,/júst a féw yárds awáy from the búll.//He was dréssed in a spléndid cóstume.'//
15 'Thát must have been véry impréssive,'/Bób sáid.//

'I súppose it wás,'/Álec ánswered.//'The tróuble wás/that the póor mán dídn't knów múch abóut búllfighting.//The búll went áfter him/befóre he éven mánaged to gét his párachute óff.//He spent móst of his tíme in the áir!'//

Answer these questions

A. 1 Didn't Alec return to work last Monday?
2 He had been on holiday, hadn't he?
3 Hadn't he been to Spain?
4 He'd been there for three weeks, hadn't he?
5 He did enjoy himself, didn't he?
6 Did he see a bullfight?
7 Was the bullfight funny?
8 The bullfighter was a showman, wasn't he?
9 He wasn't a very good bullfighter, was he?

B. 10 Who returned to work last Monday?
11 Who had been to Spain?
12 Who thought the bullfight was funny?
13 Who arrived at the ring in a helicopter?

C. 14 Had Alec been on holiday, or had he been abroad on business?

84

15 Had Alec been to Spain or Jamaica?
16 Did Alec stay in Spain for three weeks or for three months?
17 Did the bullfighter arrive at the ring in an aeroplane or a helicopter?
18 Was the man a good bullfighter, or was he just a showman?

D. 19 When did Alec return to work?
20 Where had Alec been?
21 How long had Alec spent there?
22 What did Alec see in Spain?
23 How did he find the bullfight?
24 Why did Alec call the bullfighter a showman?
25 How was the bullfighter dressed?
26 What happened to the bullfighter?

E. Mixed questions (Recorded)

F. Ask these questions
  Ask me
1a if Alec had been to Spain.
 b where he had been.
2a if he had been there for three weeks.
 b how long he had been there.
3a if he went swimming every day.
 b how often he went swimming.
4a if he found the bullfight funny.
 b why he found the bullfight funny.

G. Oral reproduction and free expression
1 Conduct the dialogue between Alec and Bob.
2 Place yourself in Alec's position. Give an account of how you spent your holiday.
3 Which countries have you visited or would you like to visit? What interesting things or events would you expect to see in these countries?

An Unwelcome Visitor

The dóorbell ráng/and Mrs Cárson ópened the frónt dóor.//Her héart sánk when she sáw Mrs Búrbidge.//Whenéver Mrs Búrbidge cálled,/she stáyed for hóurs and hóurs.//

'Góod afternóon, Mrs Cárson,'/Mrs Búrbidge sáid.//'I was júst
5 pássing/and I thóught I'd dróp ín to sáy hulló.'//

'How véry thoughtful of you,'/Mrs Cárson replíed.//'Dó cóme ín.'//

Júst as Mrs Cárson had féared,/Mrs Búrbidge stáyed for séveral hóurs.//It was néarly síx o'clóck/and Mr Cárson would be hóme from wórk sóon.//He cóuldn't stánd Mrs Búrbidge.//Mrs Cárson
10 képt wóndering/hów she could persuáde Mrs Búrbidge to léave/ withóut offénding her.//

'Hás your húsband got hóme from wórk yét?'/Mrs Cárson ásked.//

'Óh, yés,'/Mrs Búrbidge ánswered.//'He álways gets hóme about fíve o'clóck.'//

15 'It's néarly síx o'clóck.//Wón't he be gétting wórried aboút you?'/ Mrs Cárson sáid.//

'I thóught of thát,'/Mrs Búrbidge sáid,/'but it's só pléasant hére.// We've had súch a lóvely afternóon.//You knów what I'll dó?// I'll ríng up my húsband/and téll hím to cóme róund, tóo.//Máy
20 I úse your phóne pléase?'//

Answer these questions

A. 1 Didn't Mrs Carson open the front door?
  2 Mrs Burbidge was at the door, wasn't she?
  3 Was Mrs Carson pleased to see her?
  4 Didn't Mrs Carson ask Mrs Burbidge to come in?
  5 Mrs Burbidge stayed for a long time, didn't she?
  6 Did Mr Carson like Mrs Burbidge?
  7 He couldn't stand her, could he?
  8 Couldn't Mrs Carson get rid of her visitor?
  9 Mrs Burbidge wouldn't go, would she?
  10 She was going to ask her husband to come as well, wasn't she?

B. 11 Who opened the front door?
  12 Who was at the door?
  13 Who wants to use the telephone?
  14 Who will ring up Mr Burbidge?

C. 15 Was Mrs Carson pleased to see Mrs Burbidge, or was she disappointed?

16 Did Mrs Burbidge stay for a few minutes, or did she stay the whole afternoon?

17 Did Mrs Carson want Mrs Burbidge to leave, or did she want her to stay?

18 Did Mr Carson like Mrs Burbidge, or did he dislike her?

19 Is Mrs Burbidge going to ring up her husband, or is she going home?

D. 20 Why was Mrs Carson disappointed when Mrs Burbidge called?

21 When does Mr Carson come home from work?

22 How does Mr Carson feel about Mrs Burbidge?

23 How did Mrs Carson try to get Mrs Burbidge to leave?

24 Why did Mrs Burbidge decide to telephone her husband?

E. Mixed questions (Recorded)

F. Ask these questions

Ask me

1a if Mrs Carson was displeased to see Mrs Burbidge.

b why she was displeased.

2a if Mrs Burbidge stayed for several hours.

b how long she stayed.

3a if Mr Carson would return soon.

b when he would return.

4a if Mrs Carson could persuade Mrs Burbidge to leave.

b why she couldn't persuade Mrs Burbidge to leave.

G. Oral reproduction and free expression

1 Conduct the conversation between the two women.

2 Describe what happened when Mrs Burbidge called.

3 Discuss the advantages and disadvantages of having neighbours.

87

36 It Makes a Change

Mŕ and Mŕs Hóward/récently móved to a néw hóuse.//The gárden had been só neglécted/that they decíded to emplóy a gárdener.// Óne dáy,/when her húsband was at wórk,/Mŕs Hóward ásked a lócal gárdener to cóme and sée the gárden.//Áfter the mán had
5 been óver the pláce thóroughly,/Mŕs Hóward wént óut to spéak to him.//
'Hów does it lóok?'/she ásked.//
'It's been térribly neglécted, Mŕs Hóward,'/the gárdener sáid.// 'Thóse róse búshes néed prúning.//The láwn néeds cútting/and
10 the hédges néed trímming.//And ás you can/sée/the whóle gárden's fúll of wéeds.'//
'Whén can you begín wórk?'/Mŕs Hóward ásked.//
'Nót untíl néxt wéek, Mŕs Hóward,'/the gárdener sáid.//'I'm véry búsy.'//
15 'Cán't you stárt on Sáturday?'/Mŕs Hóward ásked.//
'I'm afráid nót,'/the gárdener replíed.//'I néver wórk dúring the wéek-end.//I néed a chánge after wórking in gárdens áll the wéek.'//
'I'm súre you dó,'/Mŕs Hóward sáid.//'Éveryone should háve a
20 hóbby.//Whát do you dó in your spáre tíme?'//
'I've gót a gárden of my ówn,'/the mán sáid.//'I'm ónly frée to wórk in it dúring the wéek-end.'//

Answer these questions
A. 1 Didn't Mr and Mrs Howard move to a new house recently?
2 The garden was extremely neglected, wasn't it?
3 Didn't they have to employ a gardener?
4 The gardener went over the place thoroughly, didn't he?
5 Don't the rose bushes need pruning?
6 The lawn does need cutting doesn't it?
7 Do the hedges need trimming?
8 Can the gardener begin work on Saturday?
9 Doesn't he work during the week-end?
10 Hasn't he got a garden of his own?

B. 11 Who had to employ a gardener?
12 Who said that the garden had been neglected?

13 Who will begin work next week?

C. 14 Was the Howards' garden well cared-for, or had it been neglected?

15 Would the Howards do all their own gardening, or would they employ a gardener?

16 Can the gardener begin work this week or next week?

17 Has the gardener got a hobby, or does he work all the time?

D. 18 Why did the Howards decide to employ a gardener?

19 What did the gardener do when he arrived at the Howards' house?

20 When can the gardener begin work?

21 Why can't he begin work until next week?

22 When does the gardener work in his own garden?

23 What is the gardener's hobby?

E. Mixed questions

F. Ask these questions

Ask me

1a if the Howards moved to a new house.

b when they moved to a new house.

2a if they had to employ a gardener.

b why they had to employ a gardener.

3a if the gardener can begin work soon.

b when the gardener can begin work.

4a if everyone should have a hobby.

b why everyone should have a hobby.

G. Oral reproduction and free expression

1 Conduct the conversation between Mrs Howard and the gardener.

2 Put yourself in the position of the gardener. Describe how you found Mrs Howard's garden and how you spend your time.

3 Give an account of your favourite hobby.

89

37 A Message From Nowhere

The Róbinsons were expécting guésts for dínner.//The guésts,/who were áll cólleagues of Mŕ Róbinson,/were dúe to arríve at síx-thírty.// It was a quárter pást séven/but they stíll hádn't appéared.//
    'I wónder whát has háppened to them,'/Mŕs Róbinson ásked her
5   húsband.//'Díd you téll them hów to gét here?'//
    'Of cóurse I díd,'/Mŕ Róbinson replíed.//'I sént them détailed instrúctions and enclósed a skétch-máp.'//
    'Perháps they hád an áccident,'/Mŕs Róbinson suggésted.//'Wére they cóming by cár?'//
10 'As fár as Í knów,'/Mŕ Róbinson sáid.//
    Súddenly the télephone ráng/and Mŕs Róbinson rán to ánswer it.// 'Bíll!'/she cálled./'You're wánted on the phóne!'//
    Mŕ Róbinson pícked úp the recéiver.//
    'Ís that yóu Bíll?'/a vóice sáid.//'I'm sórry we're láte.//We've lóst
15 our wáy.//We tóok a wróng túrning about tén míles báck.//I'm rínging from a públic cáll-bóx in a smáll víllage.'//
    'Whát's the náme of the víllage?'/Mŕ Róbinson ásked.//
    'Thát's the tróuble,'/the vóice sáid.//'We dón't knów.//Thís víllage dóesn't séem to be márked on the máp.'//

Answer these questions
A. 1 Weren't the Robinsons expecting guests for dinner?
      2 The guests were colleagues of Mr Robinson, weren't they?
      3 Had they arrived on time?
      4 Didn't Mr Robinson send them detailed instructions?
      5 He enclosed a sketch-map too, didn't he?
      6 The guests were coming by car, weren't they?
      7 Did the telephoné ring?
      8 Is Mr Robinson wanted on the phone?
      9 Were the guests ringing from a small village?
      10 They don't know the name of the village, do they?

B. 11 Who was expecting visitors?
      12 Who sent them detailed information and a sketch-map?
      13 Who answered the telephone?
      14 Who is wanted on the phone?

C. 15 Were the Robinsons expecting guests for dinner or for lunch?

16 Were the guests due to arrive at six-thirty or at eight-thirty?

17 Were they coming by car or by train?

18 Is Mr Robinson wanted on the phone or is his wife wanted on the phone?

19 Were the guests ringing from a small village or a large town?

20 Were they ringing from a public call-box or a private house?

D. 21 When were the guests due to arrive?

22 What information had Mr Robinson sent them?

23 Why was Mrs Robinson worried?

24 Why were the guests late?

25 Why didn't they know the name of the village?

E. Mixed questions (Recorded)

F. Ask these questions

Ask me

1a if the guests were due to arrive at six-thirty.

b when they were due to arrive.

2a if it was a quarter to seven.

b what time it was.

3a if Mr Robinson sent them detailed instructions.

b what he sent them.

4a if the telephone rang.

b when the telephone rang.

5a if he is ringing from a public call-box.

b where he is ringing from.

6a if the village is marked on the map.

b why it isn't marked on the map.

G. Oral reproduction and free expression

1 Conduct the conversation between Mr Robinson and his wife.

2 Conduct the telephone conversation between Mr Robinson and the guest.

3 Describe occasions when you have lost your way in a strange place.

to carry — llevar, conducir, acarrear,
tener consigo ; contener ; incluir, com-
38 Baby-sitting *prender ; implicar ;*
dirigir ; impulsar, mover

Befóre she léft,/Mrs Sóames gave lást mínute instrúctions to the báby-
sítter,/a yóung gírl of séventéen.//The gírl had néver dóne báby-sítting
befóre/and Mrs Sóames was a líttle ánxious.//
    'Máke yourself cómfortable, Cárol,'/Mrs Sóames sáid.//'I've
5 prepáred a tráy of fóod for you.//It's ón the táble.//You cán, of
cóurse, lísten to the rádio/or lóok at the télevision,/but dón't have it
ón tóo lóud/because you míght wáke our líttle bóy.// Sóund cárries
térribly in thís hóuse.//If the bóy wákes úp,/gó to his róom and stáy
there for a féw mínutes.//He'll gó back to sléep immédiately.//Ányway,/
10 he's fóur yéars óld,/so you shóuldn't háve any tróuble.//My húsband
and Í will be báck at about éleven o'clóck.'//
    Mr and Mrs Sóames retúrned ráther láter than they had expécted.//
A líght was stíll ón in the líving-róom/and the télevision could júst
be héard. Mrs Sóames wént to the líving-róom immédiately/ and
15 cáme out agáin a móment láter hólding the bóy.//
    'Whát was hé dóing thére?'/Mr Sóames excláimed.//'Hé's wíde
awáke.'//
    'He was lóoking at the télevision,'/Mrs Sóames sáid.//
    'Whére's Cárol?'/Mr Sóames ásked.//
20   'She's stíll in the líving-róom.//She's fást asléep!'//

Answer these questions
  A. 1 Did Mrs Soames employ a baby-sitter?
      2 The baby-sitter was a young girl, wasn't she?
      3 Had the girl ever done any baby-sitting before?
      4 Was Mrs Soames a little anxious?
      5 Can Carol look at the television?
      6 She mustn't have it on too loud, must she?
      7 She might wake up the little boy, mightn't she?
      8 Will Mr and Mrs Soames be back by 11.0 o'clock?
      9 Was Carol in the living-room when they returned?
     10 Was the boy awake?
     11 Carol's fast asleep, isn't she?

  B. 12 Who is going to baby-sit for Mrs Soames?
     13 Who has prepared a tray of food for the baby-sitter?
     14 Who will be back by 11.0 o'clock?

15 Who was looking at the television when Mr and Mrs Soames returned?

C. 16 Was the baby-sitter a young girl or an old lady?
17 Will Carol sit in the living-room or in the dining-room?
18 Is the little boy four years old or two years old?
19 Was the boy asleep or awake when the Soames returned?
20 Was he looking at the television or listening to the radio?
21 Was Carol asleep or awake when the Soames returned?

D. 22 Why was Mrs Soames anxious about the baby-sitter?
23 How old is Carol?
24 What had Mrs Soames prepared for her?
25 Why mustn't Carol have the television on too loud?
26 When did the Soames expect to be home?
27 What did Mrs Soames find when she got home?

E. Mixed questions (Recorded)

F. Ask these questions
   Ask me
1a if Mrs Soames was a little anxious.
 b why she was a little anxious.
2a if the little boy is four years old.
 b how old the little boy is.
3a if the Soames returned late.
 b when they returned.
4a if the boy was looking at the television.
 b what the boy was doing.

G. Oral reproduction and free expression
1 Give an account of what happened from the time Mrs Soames gave the baby-sitter instructions.
2 Give an account of what might have happened during the absence of Mr and Mrs Soames.
3 Give reasons why baby-sitting can sometimes be very difficult.

39 Monday Morning

Mónday mórning/is álways the wórst mórning/of the wéek.//Éverybody is sléepy;//éverybody is bád-témpered;//éverybody is in a húrry.//Lást Mónday/was éven wórse than úsual.//

'Húrry úp, Díck!'/fáther shóuted/as he bánged on the báthroom
5 dóor.//'I've gót a tráin to cátch!'//

'I'm sháving,'/Díck ánswered.//'I'll be óut in a mínute.'//

'Bréakfast's réady,'/móther cálled from the kítchen.//As she gót no replý,/she cáme úpstáirs to sée what was góing ón.//'Whére's Dávid?'/ she ásked.//'Ís he stíll in béd?'//She knócked at his bédroom dóor
10 lóudly.//'You'd bétter gét up,'/she cálled.// 'It's a quárter to éight.// Your bréakfast's gétting cóld!'//

'I dón't féel like ány bréakfast,'/Dávid múmbled.//'I'll have anóther fíve mínutes sléep instéad.'//

Móther was abóut to gó into his róom/and drág him óut of béd/
15 when the dóorbéll ráng.//She húrried dównstáirs/to ópen the dóor.// It was the póstman.//

'Góod morning, Mrs Cráwford,'/he sáid chéerfully.//'It's a lóvely dáy, ísn't it?'//

'You wóuldn't thínk so if you líved hére,'/móther ánswered.//'Ón
20 Móndays/thís pláce is líke a mádhouse.'//

Answer these questions

A. 1 Isn't Monday morning the worst morning of the week?
2 Last Monday was even worse than usual, wasn't it?
3 Father catches a train, doesn't he?
4 Is Dick shaving?
5 Won't he be out in a minute?
6 Isn't David still in bed?
7 Hadn't he better get up?
8 He'd rather stay in bed, wouldn't he?
9 Won't he stay in bed for another five minutes?
10 Didn't the doorbell ring?
11 It was the postman, wasn't it?

B. 12 Who is in the bathroom?
13 Who wants to go to the bathroom?
14 Who's still in bed?

94

15 Who rang the doorbell?

C. 16 Is Dick in the bathroom or in his bedroom?
17 Is he shaving or having a bath?
18 Had mother been preparing breakfast, or had she been making the beds?
19 Has David got up, or is he still in bed?
20 Did someone knock at the front door or at the back door?
21 Was it the postman or the baker?

D. 22 Why was father in a hurry?
23 Where was Dick?
24 What was he doing?
25 Where's David?
26 Why did mother come upstairs?
27 Why doesn't David want to get up?
28 Why did mother have to go downstairs?
29 What did the postman say to her?

E. Mixed questions (Recorded)

F. Ask these questions
   Ask me
1a   if father's in a hurry.
 b   why he's in a hurry.
2a   if David wants to get up.
 b   why he doesn't want to get up.
3a   if mother hurried downstairs.
 b   why she hurried downstairs.
4a   if it was the postman.
 b   who it was.

G. Oral reproduction and free expression
 1 Describe the scene last Monday morning.
 2 'There are certain days when everything seems to go wrong.' What is your experience?

40 Look Where You're Going!

One thíng that has álways impréssed me aboút the Pálace Hotél/is the lóng líne of gláss dóors/at the éntrance.//The lást tíme I stáyed there,/ I gót a surpríse/because some wórkmen/were stícking úgly bánds of góld tápe/on the gláss dóors.//

5 'Whát are you dóing thát fór?'/I ásked óne of the wórkmen.//'You will spóil the appéarance of the búilding!'//

'We've been órdered to stíck thís tápe ón,'/a wórkman ánswered,/ 'becáuse só mány péople/trý to wálk thróugh thése dóors.//Lást yéar/séveral résidents were sériously ínjured/and fíve of the dóors

10 were bróken.'//

'I dón't belíeve it,'/I sáid.//'Anyone can sée a gláss dóor.//Whý,/ thát's the fírst thíng you nótice about thís búilding.'//

'You'd be surprísed at the númber of péople/who dón't éven nótice/ that thése dóors are máde of gláss,'/the wórkman ánswered.//

15 'I've néver héard of such nónsense!'/I excláimed.//

Súddenly,/there was a lóud crásh/a féw yárds awáy from us.//Súre enóugh,/an unfórtunate vísitor/had wálked stráight ínto óne of the gláss dóors!//He was rúbbing his fórehead/and stáring ángrily/at the gláss dóor in frónt of hím.//

20 'You sée whát I méan!'/the wórkman sáid.//

Answer these questions

A. 1 You've always liked the entrance to the Palace Hotel, haven't you?
2 Didn't you get a surprise last time you stayed there?
3 Were some workmen removing the doors?
4 Would they spoil the appearance of the building?
5 They were sticking bands of gold tape on the doors, weren't they?
6 Weren't you surprised?
7 Had a number of residents at the hotel been injured?
8 Did you hear a loud crash?

B. 9 Who was sticking bands of gold tape on the glass doors?
10 Who was seriously injured last year?
11 Who heard a loud crash?

96

C. 12 Were the workmen sticking bands of gold tape on the doors, or were they painting them?

13 Did you think they would spoil or improve the appearance of the building?

14 Did you believe the workman when he told you that a number of people failed to notice the glass doors, or did you disbelieve him?

15 Was there a loud crash a few yards away from you, or was there an explosion?

16 Had a visitor walked into a door, or had he fallen over?

D. 17 What has always impressed you about the Palace Hotel?

18 Where were the workmen sticking the gold tape?

19 What did you feel about this?

20 Why were the workmen sticking the tape on the doors?

21 How would the gold tape prevent people from walking into the doors?

22 When did you believe what the workman had told you?

E. Mixed questions (Recorded)

F. Ask these questions

Ask me

1a if some workmen were sticking gold tape on the doors.

b what they were doing that for.

2a if many of the residents fail to notice the glass doors.

b what many of the residents fail to notice.

3a if there had been a number of accidents.

b why there had been a number of accidents

G. Oral reproduction and free expression

1 Conduct the dialogue between the workman and the resident.

2 Describe in detail why you got a surprise on your last visit to the Palace Hotel.

3 What common household objects can be dangerous to children? Explain why they can be dangerous.

Chapter 6
TO THE TEACHER

Summary of Question Forms

A. Mixed questions
These will involve most of the forms learnt so far.

B. Mixed questions (Recorded)

C. Asking questions
The questions to be asked will *not* be presented in pairs.

D. Oral reproduction and free expression

41   The Balkan Express

The first person I saw as soon as I returned from my holidays was my grandfather. He opened the front door for me and stood there, looking me up and down in amazement.

'Whatever's the matter with you?' he asked.

5   I went straight into the living-room and sank exhausted into an armchair. I was hard put to explain my appearance. I was pale, unshaven, dirty and tired out after my journey.

'I've been travelling on the Balkan Express,' I mumbled weakly, 'and I haven't eaten a thing for over eighteen hours. As I didn't get
10 a seat, I spent most of my time in the corridor where I was nearly trampled to death.'

'The Balkan Express!' my grandfather exclaimed. 'When I was a young man, that was a wonderful train. There was a permanent dining-car and you could get some of the best food and wines in
15 Europe. I can even remember a time when a gypsy orchestra was employed to play to the passengers during meal-times.' He looked me up and down again, then added with a sigh, 'You couldn't beat the old Balkan Express for comfort.'

'Times have changed, grandfather,' I said sadly.

20   'Judging from your appearance, my boy,' he answered, 'they've changed for the worse. Now you go and have a nice hot bath, and I'll get you something warm to drink.'

Answer these questions

A. 1 Who was the first person you saw when you returned from your holidays?
2 Was your grandfather surprised when he saw you?
3 Why was he surprised?
4 Did you go into the living-room?
5 Weren't you exhausted?
6 Why did you feel so tired?
7 What did you tell your grandfather?
8 How long had you been travelling on the Balkan Express?
9 You didn't have a comfortable journey, did you?
10 What was your grandfather's opinion of the Balkan Express?
11 Had your grandfather travelled on the Balkan Express when he was a young man?

12 Was the food on the train good in the old days?
13 Could your grandfather remember the train well?
14 Were the passengers provided with any entertainment on the old Balkan Express?
15 What sort of entertainment did they have?
16 Has the train service improved since then, or has it got worse?
17 What did your grandfather tell you to do?
18 What did he offer to get you?

B. Mixed questions (Recorded)

C. Ask these questions
Ask me
1 who I first saw when I returned from my holidays.
2 whether I had been on holiday.
3 whether my grandfather opened the door for me.
4 why my grandfather was so surprised.
5 what I looked like.
6 whether I wasn't tired after my journey.
7 where I had been.
8 how long I went without food.
9 why I didn't get a seat.
10 whether I had to stand.
11 what the Balkan Express was like in my grandfather's time.
12 what my grandfather told me to do.

D. Oral reproduction and free expression
1 Conduct the dialogue between grandfather and yourself adding as much new information as you can.
2 Explain why (according to the passage) the Balkan Express has changed for the worse.
3 Discuss the advantages and disadvantages of the following means of transport: cars, trains, ships and aeroplanes.

42 Boys Will be Boys

On Saturday morning, the postman delivered a large parcel for Tommy. The parcel contained a birthday present and it had arrived just in time.

Tommy looked at the stamps on the packet. 'It's from Uncle Bill,'
5 he shouted excitedly. Even though Uncle Bill was in America, he had not forgotten Tommy's birthday. Mother made Tommy promise not to open the parcel until the following day.

'Your birthday's not till tomorrow,' she said. 'You should open it in the morning together with your other presents.'

10 The next day, father was just as excited as Tommy when they discovered that the parcel contained an electric train set. 'Let's go upstairs and put it together,' father said.

Tommy remained with his father for about an hour but finally got bored with the train set and went into the living-room to see the
15 rest of his presents.

At about lunch time, Tommy's mother came into the living-room. 'Where's your father?' she asked. 'I've been looking for him everywhere.'

'He's upstairs, Mum,' Tommy answered. 'He put my train set
20 together this morning and he's been playing with it ever since!'

Answer these questions

A. 1 When did the postman deliver the parcel?
2 Who was it for?
3 Whose birthday was it?
4 What was the first thing Tommy looked at?
5 Where had the parcel come from?
6 It arrived just in time, didn't it?
7 What did mother make Tommy promise?
8 Why did she make Tommy promise not to open the parcel until the following day?
9 When did Tommy open the parcel?
10 Did the parcel contain a model car?
11 What did it contain?
12 Who went upstairs with Tommy?
13 Why did they go upstairs?

14 How long did Tommy stay with his father?
15 Didn't Tommy get bored with the train set?
16 Where were the rest of Tommy's presents?
17 Tommy wanted to see them, didn't he?
18 Did Tommy stay with his father, or did he go downstairs?
19 Did Tommy's mother come into the living-room?
20 Has she been looking for her husband?
21 Where is her husband?
22 What is he doing with the train set?

B. Mixed questions (Recorded)

C. Ask these questions
   Ask me
   1 if there was a parcel for Tommy.
   2 who the parcel was for.
   3 how Tommy found out that the parcel had come from America.
   4 who the parcel was from.
   5 if he forgot Tommy's birthday.
   6 when Tommy can open the parcel.
   7 if it is Tommy's birthday today.
   8 if he has any other presents.
   9 what the parcel contained.
   10 if Tommy's father wanted to put it together.
   11 why Tommy came downstairs.
   12 what Tommy's father has been doing.
   13 why his wife hasn't been able to find him.
   14 what he is playing with.

D. Oral reproduction and free expression
   1 Describe what happened from the time the parcel arrived.
   2 Conduct a short discussion on this subject: Which toys are most suitable for young children?

43 Well Worth the Money

While walking through the park, we stopped by the pond to watch some children who were sailing model boats. There were so many boats in the pond that morning that quite a few people had gathered on the banks to see them.

5   Suddenly, someone shouted, 'There's a man in the pond!' We looked up and sure enough, a man's head could just be seen on the other side of the pond. The man appeared to be swimming vigorously and was coming straight towards us.

'He must be crazy,' a young man said. 'I wouldn't dive into that
10 pond for a fortune. And anyway, it must be freezing cold.'

The brackish water of the pond was certainly not inviting. As it was still early March, the water must certainly have been very cold.

After a short time, the man approached the bank. The water was very shallow, so he walked the last few yards. We were astonished
15 to see that he was fully dressed.

'Nice swim?' the young man asked.

'Nice swim, my foot!' the man remarked irritably. 'It's freezing. I did it for a bet!'

Answer these questions

A. 1 Were you in the park?
2 Didn't you stop by the pond?
3 Why did you stop there?
4 You weren't the only one standing near the pond, were you?
5 Didn't someone see a man in the pond?
6 Was the man at the other side of the pond?
7 What was he doing?
8 The man was swimming towards you, wasn't he?
9 Was the water warm?
10 It was freezing cold, wasn't it?
11 Why wasn't it very inviting?
12 What season of the year was it?
13 The man came near the bank, didn't he?
14 Was the water near the bank very deep?
15 Why was the man able to walk the last few yards?
16 Why was everyone surprised at the man?

17 The man wasn't wearing a bathing costume, was he?
18 Had the man enjoyed his swim?
19 Was the man pleased or irritable?
20 Why did the man swim across the pond?

B. Mixed questions (Recorded)

C. Ask these questions
   Ask me
   1 where we were.
   2 why we stopped near the pond.
   3 if we were the only people there.
   4 if there was a man in the pond.
   5 if he was swimming.
   6 if the young man would dive into the pond.
   7 why the young man wasn't willing to dive into the pond.
   8 whether the water was very cold.
   9 when the swimmer stood up.
   10 why everyone was surprised.
   11 if the man had enjoyed his swim.
   12 why he didn't enjoy his swim.
   13 why he did it.
   14 if he felt pleased with himself.
   15 if he would get any money for swimming across the pond.

D. Oral reproduction and free expression
   1 Describe what happened when you stopped by the pond.
   2 Put yourself in the swimmer's position. Explain in detail how
     you came to swim across the pond.
   3 Describe an occasion when you have won or lost a bet.

44 Future Prospects

From Ernest's point of view, the interview was going very well indeed.
Six days before, he had applied for a job with a small business company
and now he was being interviewed by one of the directors. The
advertisement had invited applications from ambitious young men
5 who would be willing to travel abroad at short notice if necessary
and who would not mind working irregular hours. Ernest had taken
great pains not to say anything silly and the director seemed to be
most impressed.

'You say, you're not married Mr Reeves,' the director said.

10 'No, sir,' Ernest answered. 'I'm getting married next June, but
I'm sure my future wife won't have any objection to my keeping
irregular hours.'

'I see from your application form you have worked as a salesman
for two years. Why do you wish to change your job now?'

15 'I found the work too dull, sir,' Ernest answered.

'That's a refreshing change,' the director said. 'Most young men
these days seem to want dull jobs. The first question young men ask
me is whether the job I'm offering carries a pension. They want to
retire before they start!'

20 'Does the job carry a pension, sir?' Ernest asked anxiously.

Answer these questions
   A.   1 Was Ernest being interviewed for a job?
2 Was Ernest pleased with the way the interview was going?
3 When had he applied for this job?
4 Was this a small or a large business company?
5 Who interviewed Ernest?
6 Had this job been advertised?
7 Will the young men who are appointed have to travel abroad?
8 They'll have to work irregular hours too, won't they?
9 Did the director seem to be impressed with Ernest?
10 Who asked Ernest if he was married?
11 Was Ernest married?
12 When is Ernest getting married?
13 Will his future wife object to his keeping irregular hours?
14 What did the director learn from Ernest's application form?

15 How long had Ernest worked as a salesman?
16 He wants to change his job now, doesn't he?
17 Why does he want to change his job?
18 Was the director pleased with Ernest's answer?
19 Why was the director pleased?
20 What, according to the director, is the first question most young men ask when they apply for a job?
21 Didn't Ernest ask the same question?

B. Mixed questions (Recorded)

C. Ask these questions
   Ask me
   1 if Ernest is being interviewed for a job.
   2 when he applied for it.
   3 who he is being interviewed by.
   4 whether it is a large company.
   5 whether Ernest is ambitious.
   6 whether he would be willing to travel abroad.
   7 if he will have to work irregular hours.
   8 why the director seemed to be impressed.
   9 when Ernest is getting married.
   10 whether his future wife will object to his keeping irregular hours.
   11 what Ernest's previous job was.
   12 why Ernest wished to change his job.
   13 how long he had worked as a salesman.
   14 if the job carries a pension.
   15 what Ernest wants to know.

D. Oral reproduction and free expression
   1 Conduct the interview between Ernest and the company director. Imagine how the interview was concluded.
   2 Describe your own experiences with interviews.
   3 Can a prospective employer learn very much from an interview? Conduct a short discussion on this subject.

45 Guests for Dinner

At a quarter to six, Mrs Alison heard her husband park the car outside the house and immediately went out to speak to him.

'What's the matter, darling?' he asked. 'You look upset.'

'I've made a terrible mistake, Jim,' she said. 'Mrs Johnson rang me
5 up about half an hour ago. We got talking and then without thinking, I asked her and her husband to come and have dinner with us this evening.'

'Well, that's nothing to get upset about!' Mr Alison said. 'We should have a pleasant evening. We haven't seen the Johnsons for
10 ages.'

'I'd like them to come,' replied Mrs Alison, 'but I've just discovered there's hardly any food in the house. You didn't by any chance remember to buy some steak? I asked you to get some on your way home from work three days ago.'

15 'Steak?' Mr Alison said. 'Good heavens, yes. I remember now. As a matter of fact I did get some. You ought to have reminded me about it. It's in the boot of the car. It's been there for the past three days!'

Answer these questions

A. 1 What time did Mr Alison get home from work?
2 How did Mrs Alison know her husband had arrived?
3 Where did Mr Alison park his car?
4 Didn't Mrs Alison go out to meet him?
5 She looked upset, didn't she?
6 Did her husband notice this?
7 Why was Mrs Alison upset?
8 Who rang Mrs Alison up?
9 How long ago did Mrs Johnson ring her up?
10 Who invited the Johnsons to dinner?
11 When will the Johnsons come to dinner?
12 Was Mr Alison sorry to hear this?
13 Have Mr and Mrs Alison seen the Johnsons recently?
14 Why is Mrs Alison sorry she asked them to come?
15 Has Mrs Alison prepared a meal for her guests?
16 Why hasn't she prepared a meal for her guests?

17 Had she asked her husband to get some steak?
18 How long ago was this?
19 Did he get any steak?
20 Did his wife remind him about the steak?
21 Where is the steak?
22 How long has it been there?

B. Mixed questions (Recorded)

C. Ask these questions
Ask me
1 what time Mr Alison got home from work.
2 whether Mrs Alison heard him.
3 why she went out to speak to her husband.
4 if she looks upset.
5 if she's made a mistake.
6 when Mrs Johnson rang her up.
7 who Mrs Alison invited to dinner.
8 whether the Johnsons will be coming to dinner.
9 if Mr Alison was pleased to hear this.
10 if they have seen the Johnsons recently.
11 why Mrs Alison can't prepare a meal for them.
12 if Mr Alison remembered to get some steak.
13 how long ago this was.
14 where the steak was.
15 how long it had been in the boot of the car.

D. Oral reproduction and free expression
1 Conduct the conversation between Mrs Alison and her husband.
2 Imagine that the Johnsons turned up for dinner. How do you imagine they spent the evening?
3 Describe any enjoyable evening you have spent with friends.

46 Back in Fashion

Millie stopped outside a shoe-shop and looked in the window. For some time, she gazed at a pair of fur-lined high boots on display. 'They're exactly what I've been looking for,' she thought. The boots were unpriced, so Millie decided to inquire how much they cost.

5   'I'd like to buy a pair of boots like the ones you have in the window,' she asked the shop-assistant. 'Could you tell me how much they are please?'

As the price was reasonable, Millie decided to try a pair on. The shop-assistant asked her to sit down and brought a pair. While she

10 was helping Millie to put them on, she kept looking at Millie's stockings. Millie was wearing a pair of stockings made of fine white lace.

'Excuse my asking,' the shop-assistant said at last, 'but where did you get those stockings? We've been trying to obtain stockings like

15 these for some time. They're the very latest fashion and they're in great demand.'

'They're pretty, aren't they?' Millie said. 'I was given them by my grandmother.'

Answer these questions
   A.   1 Didn't Millie stop outside a shoe-shop?
        2 She looked in the window, didn't she?
        3 What was she looking at?
        4 Was she looking at a pair of high-heeled shoes?
        5 Why did Millie go into the shop?
        6 She didn't know how much the boots cost, did she?
        7 Who did she speak to in the shoe-shop?
        8 What did Millie want to know?
        9 Were the boots too expensive for Millie to buy?
     10 Didn't Millie want to try them on?
     11 Who helped Millie to put the boots on?
     12 What did the shop-assistant keep looking at?
     13 What were Millie's stockings made of?
     14 What did the shop-assistant want to know?
     15 Were stockings like these obtainable in the shop?
     16 They were the very latest fashion, weren't they?

17 Weren't they in great demand?
18 Had Millie bought these stockings?
19 Was she given them?
20 The stockings were a present, weren't they?
21 Who had given them to Millie?

B. Mixed questions (Recorded)

C. Ask these questions
Ask me
1 what Millie was looking at.
2 what she could see in the window.
3 whether the boots were fur-lined.
4 if that was what she had been looking for.
5 whether Millie knew the price of the boots.
6 how much the boots cost.
7 if Millie would like to buy them.
8 if the shop-assistant could tell her how much they cost.
9 if they weren't very expensive.
10 if Millie would try a pair on.
11 where Millie sat down.
12 if the assistant brought her a pair of boots.
13 what the assistant kept looking at.
14 what Millie was wearing.
15 what the stockings were made of.
16 if Millie had been given them.

D. Oral reproduction and free expression
1 Describe what happened after Millie stopped outside the shoe-shop.
2 Conduct the conversation between Millie and the shop-assistant.
3 Conduct a short discussion on this subject: Women's Fashions.

47   Blackmail

The great liner had anchored some distance from the harbour. The captain had told the passengers that they could visit the port if they wished to, but they must be on board at 5.30 as the ship would set sail at 6 o'clock. The ship was far too big to dock in the harbour and
5 all day long local boatmen had been rowing to and from the liner carrying sightseers to the small port.

At about 5 o'clock, Miss Merryweather hired a local boatman to take her back to the ship. The man had asked for $5 which Miss Merryweather thought excessive.
10 'Either you accept $3, or I shall hire another boatman,' Miss Merryweather said firmly.

After a good deal of arguing, the man reluctantly agreed to take her for $3.

When they were about two hundred yards from the liner, the
15 boatman stopped rowing. 'Is anything the matter?' inquired Miss Merryweather anxiously.

'Nothing at all,' the boatman replied. 'Either you pay me $5, or you can sit here and watch the ship sail away without you.'

Answer these questions
   A. 1 Did the liner go right into the harbour?
      2 It had anchored some distance away, hadn't it?
      3 Could the passengers visit the port if they wanted to?
      4 Who had given them permission?
      5 What time must they be on board?
      6 Will the ship sail at midnight?
      7 What time will it sail?
      8 Why didn't the ship dock in the harbour?
      9 How did the passengers get to the port?
     10 Did Miss Merryweather want to go to the shore, or did she want to get back to the ship?
     11 Did she hire a local boatman?
     12 Did the boatman ask for $50?
     13 How much did he ask for?
     14 Why wasn't Miss Merryweather prepared to pay $5?
     15 How much did she offer the boatman?

16 What did she threaten to do?
17 Did the boatman agree to take her for $3?
18 Was he satisfied with this sum?
19 Did the boatman take Miss Merryweather straight back to the ship?
20 Why did he stop rowing?
21 He wanted more money didn't he?

B. Mixed questions (Recorded)

C. Ask these questions
Ask me
1 where the ship had anchored.
2 if any of the passengers visited the port.
3 when they must be back.
4 why the ship didn't dock in the harbour.
5 who took the passengers to the port.
6 when Miss Merryweather hired a local boatman.
7 how much the man asked for.
8 why Miss Merryweather thought this was excessive.
9 whether she offered less.
10 whether they argued about the price.
11 whether the man thinks that $3 is enough.
12 why he stopped rowing.
13 if anything is the matter.
14 how much more the boatman wanted.
15 if Miss Merryweather had to get back on board.

D. Oral reproduction and free expression
1 Describe what happened after the ship anchored.
2 Conduct the conversation between Miss Merryweather and the boatman. Add as much detail as you like.
3 What do you think tourists should see in your country? Give reasons why they should see these things.

48 The Ploughboy

'What am I offered for this superb work of art?' the auctioneer asked. His assistant held up a small, dark picture for us to inspect. The buyers, all local village people, were not impressed by the auctioneer's description of the picture.

5 'Do you call that a picture?' someone asked rudely.

The auctioneer ignored the remark and waited for an offer. I looked at the catalogue. The picture was described as 'The Ploughboy' by an unknown artist. Glancing at the picture again, I noticed that it had been coated so heavily with varnish that neither a boy nor a

10 plough was visible.

'Come along,' the auctioneer said impatiently. 'I can't wait all day.'

'Five pence,' someone said.

The crowd laughed. The auctioneer glared at us sternly. 'We'll

15 have to go on to the next item,' he said.

'Fifty pence,' I said, surprised at the sound of my own voice. It was the highest offer and the picture was mine.

'You may be a lucky man,' the auctioneer said encouragingly. 'Who knows, there might be a masterpiece under all that varnish!'

Answer these questions

A. 1 Did you go to an auction?
  2 Was the auctioneer selling a picture?
  3 How did he describe it?
  4 What did the auctioneer's assistant do?
  5 The buyers were all local village people, weren't they?
  6 How did they feel about the auctioneer's description of the picture?
  7 Someone was very rude about it, wasn't he?
  8 What did he say to the auctioneer?
  9 The auctioneer didn't answer him, did he?
  10 Did you have a catalogue?
  11 How was the picture described in the catalogue?
  12 Had the picture been painted by a well-known artist, or was the artist unknown?
  13 Why was it impossible to see anything in the picture?

14 How much did someone offer for the picture?
15 Didn't the auctioneer accept this offer?
16 Wasn't the crowd amused?
17 How much did you offer for the picture?
18 Had you intended to buy it?
19 Did anyone else offer more than you did?
20 What did the auctioneer say to you when you bought the picture?

B. Mixed questions (Recorded)

C. Ask these questions
Ask me
1 if the auctioneer was trying.to sell a picture.
2 how he described it.
3 if the picture was very dark.
4 if the buyers were impressed by the auctioneer's description of the picture.
5 if someone made a rude remark about the picture.
6 why the auctioneer didn't answer him.
7 if I looked at the catalogue.
8 what the picture was called.
9 if it was by a well-known artist.
10 whether any details could be seen in the picture.
11 why the auctioneer was impatient.
12 if someone offered him five pence.
13 if the auctioneer took this offer seriously.
14 how much I bought the picture for.
15 if this was the highest offer.

D. Oral reproduction and free expression
1 Describe what happened at the auction.
2 Describe any sale you have attended.

Multiple Choice Exercises

Listen to the reading of the text, then choose the right answer A, B, C, *or* D *in each exercise.*

1 A Good Book

1 Inspector Robert Jones is looking for
   A the library   B Miss Green   C a murderer   D a good book

2 Miss Green is
   A a detective   B an inspector   C a librarian   D a murderer

3 Miss Green can't tell Inspector Robert Jones the . . . name.
   A murderer's   B detective's   C librarian's
   D inspector's

2 In the Park

1 The children are . . . in the park.
   A running   B standing   C walking   D sitting

2 They see a notice
   A on the grass   B on a tree   C near the park   D on a bench

3 What does the notice say?
   A 'Wet Grass'   B 'Wet Paint'   C 'Keep Off The Grass'
   D 'Keep Off This Bench'

3 He's not an Artist

1 Mrs Price is standing
   A in her garden   B in Mrs Robinson's garden   C upstairs
   D on her ladder

2 Mrs Robinson wants a
   A picture   B ladder   C hobby   D husband

3 Mr Robinson is painting *Price*
   A a picture   B the fence   C the bathroom   D the ladder

4 What is the Baby Doing?

1 John Wilkins goes

A upstairs   B to the kitchen   C to the living-room
D downstairs

2 The baby is in

A the kitchen   B his room   C the living-room   D the
bathroom

3 The baby is cleaning

A his teeth   B his shoes   C the bathroom   D his mother's
shoes

5 In a Department Store

1 Mrs Jenkins is

A a customer   B a shop-assistant   C a fat lady   D a store
detective

2 The fat lady is looking at

A a coat   B the counter   C the shop-assistant   D Mrs
Jenkins

3 The fat lady thinks Mrs Jenkins is going to

A leave the shop   B bring a coat   C serve her   D speak
to her

6 A Modern Picture

1 Sally paints pictures

A at home   B in her bedroom   C at school   D in an
aeroplane

2 The green lines are

A a house   B trees   C an aeroplane   D Sally's mother

3 What is *not* in Sally's picture?

A Her bedroom   B An aeroplane   C Her mother   D The
sky

7 You Can't Park Here

1 The policeman is standing behind

A his car B Mr Mason's car C a notice D Mr Mason

2 The policeman gives Mr Mason

A a ticket B a notice C a notebook D a car

3 Mr Mason says,

A 'This is my car' B 'You can't park here' C 'This car is very big' D 'This isn't my car'

8 Next-door Neighbours

1 Mr Taylor is going to

A a ship B London C Pond Street D America

2 The stranger's name is

A Taylor B Neighbour C Bennet D Hampstead

3 Mr Bennet lives at number 24 Pond Street and Mr Taylor lives

A in America B at number 23 Pond Street C at number 22 Pond Street D near Hampstead

9 Early One Morning

1 There was no petrol

A in the country B in the tank C in our town D at the garage

2 The garage was shut

A on Sundays B last Sunday C at six-thirty D after nine o'clock

3 Between six-thirty and nine o'clock the children went

A to the country B back to bed C to the garage D to sleep

10 At the Hotel

1 We wanted a room

A without a bathroom   B with two bathrooms   C on the
ground floor   D on the first floor

2 Number twenty-two was

A the stranger's room   B our room   C my wife's room
D the manager's room

3 What mistake did the manager make? He gave us

A a room on the first floor   B a room with a private bathroom
C the keys to the wrong room   D the keys to number
twenty-two

11 What's for Dinner?

1 Tim had fish

A for breakfast   B for lunch   C for dinner   D yesterday

2 The waiter brought Tim and Pat

A yesterday's menu   B today's menu   C a new menu
D a lunch menu

3 Tim did not want ... for dinner.

A vegetables   B fish   C roast beef   D peas and potatoes

12 A Clever Cat

1 Who woke up Mrs Thompson?

A The cat   B Irene   C Her husband   D The baby

2 Mr Thompson got out of bed and went to

A the door   B the window   C the garden   D the
greenhouse

3 Why can't Mr Thompson throw a stone at the cat? Because

A the cat is sitting on the greenhouse   B he can't see it
C it is not his cat   D it is not his greenhouse

13 The Daily News

1 Joe is

A a newsagent   B a workman   C Mr Green's friend   D a business man

2 Yesterday, some workmen

A robbed a bank   B robbed a factory   C changed their names and addresses   D went on strike

3 Joe thinks

A there's a lot of news today   B the weather changes every day   C the same things happen every day   D we don't read newspapers

14 At the Grocer's

1 Mrs Ford did not want

A a packet of biscuits   B a packet of tea   C a tin of tomatoes   D a tin of tomato soup

2 What did the delivery boy drop on Mrs Ford's doorstep last week?

A Eggs   B Sugar   C Flour   D Tea

3 Who will carry the eggs to Mrs Ford's house this week?

A The new delivery boy   B Mrs Ford   C The old delivery boy   D The grocer

15 Late for Work

1 At six o'clock in the evening I

A left the office   B caught a train   C had my dinner D returned home

2 This morning, the boss got to the office

A before me   B at ten o'clock   C early   D after me

3 The boss was

A late   B tired   C hungry   D angry

16 Help!

1 The woman shouted

A 'Come in!'   B 'Don't move!'   C 'Help!'   D 'Who are you?'

2 I heard a shot and

A knocked at the door   B laughed   C walked past the room
D put the gun in my pocket

3 The man and the woman were

A playing a game   B acting   C fighting   D quarrelling

17 A Pair of Glasses

1 When the optician said that tortoise-shell frames were rather dear, I

A broke his mirror   B blushed   C chose plastic ones
D crashed to the floor.

2 I broke the optician's mirror because

A I was angry   B I could not reach it   C I could not see
it very well   D it was made of plastic

3 The optician thought

A I didn't need glasses   B my wife was right   C my wife
needed glasses   D I could see very well

18 Our New Secretary

1 Who answered the telephone?

A Mr Alan Bright   B Miss Simpson   C Mr Calder   D A
salesman

2 Mr Alan Bright knew that Mr Calder was in his office when
Miss Simpson

A put her hand over the mouthpiece   B said, 'Mr Calder says
that he's not in his office'   C asked, 'What shall I say, sir?'
D said, 'I'm afraid you can't speak to Mr Calder now'

3 Mr Alan Bright could not speak to Mr Calder because

A Miss Simpson was speaking to him   B Mr Calder was not in
his office   C Mr Calder was in his office   D Mr Calder did
not want to speak to him

19 Two Tramps and a Dog

1 A dog was walking ... the tramps.

   A behind   B towards   C in front of   D beside

2 The car hit the dog because

   A it missed the tramps   B the driver did not like dogs
   C the driver could not stop it   D the dog was in the middle of
   the road

3 The tramps accepted the money

   A because the dog was not theirs   B but the dog was not
   theirs   C because they were not sorry for the dog   D but
   they were not sorry for the dog

20 The Horse Couldn't Sing

1 I enjoyed the opera performance because it was

   A funny   B short   C good   D bad

2 I left the theatre

   A when the curtain came down   B when a horse jumped off
   the stage   C at the end of the first act   D while the singers
   were still singing

3 The opera performance ended early because one horse

   A couldn't sing   B jumped off the stage   C refused to go back
   to the stage   D had to leave the theatre

21 Easy to Drive

1 The crowd wanted to look at the car because

   A it was a new model   B the salesman was trying to sell it
   C a woman could drive it   D it was standing in the street

2 The car went through the showroom window when the
   salesman

   A smiled with pleasure   B got into it   C started the engine
   D pressed a button

3 The story shows that

A only women can drive automatic cars   B the car was easy
to drive   C the car was not easy to drive   D the salesman
was not able to drive a car

22 It's Never Too Late

1 Tommy's mother was surprised because Tommy was

A inviting Aunt Lucy to his birthday party   B in his room
C thinking about his birthday   D writing a letter to Aunt
Lucy

2 Usually, Tommy writes letters

A after his birthday   B to no-one   C on his birthday
D late.

3 In his letter, Tommy was

A inviting Aunt Lucy to his birthday party   B thanking Aunt
Lucy for this year's present   C thanking Aunt Lucy for last
year's present   D asking Aunt Lucy for a present

23 The Amateur Photographer

1 The chemist looked at me sadly because

A my film was not ready   B I opened the envelope   C my
photographs were not very successful   D my sister has no legs

2 I spoilt the roll of film because

A my camera lets in light   B my camera cannot take colour
photographs   C I took the photographs myself   D I am an
amateur photographer

3 I laughed when I

A opened the envelope   B saw the rest of the photographs
C spoilt the roll of film   D left the chemist's shop

24 It's Quicker on Foot

1 Judy and Frank were waiting for the lift on the . . . floor.

A fourth   B seventh   C third   D ground

2 Frank did not want to walk to the . . . floor.

A fourth   B seventh   C third   D ground

3 Judy reached the ground floor, but the lift
A went up to the seventh floor   B was at the third floor
C reached the fourth floor   D stopped between the third and fourth floors

25 First Flight

1 The plane began to shake and rattle

A while the passengers were fastening their seat belts
B before it moved down the runway
C as it climbed into the air
D when it was in the air

2 The old lady asked for another sweet because the first one

A took her mind off the plane
B did not take her mind off the plane
C helped her to swallow
D did not help her to swallow

26 Dinner for Two

1 Max was preparing a lot of food because

A he was an expert cook
B his sister was starving
C he was expecting company
D he wanted to eat it all

2 Anne thought that there was . . . food for one person.

A not enough   B too much   C very little   D just enough

27 The Student Teacher

1 John went to Italy in order to

A get a job
B have a holiday
C teach English
D learn Italian

2 Luigi gave John

A a holiday
B pocket money
C Italian conversation lessons
D American money

28 The Bag They Missed

1 The police had heard that six thieves had

A stopped a van
B left the van near the river
C stolen a bag full of money
D climbed into the back of the van

2 The thieves took a bag of

A wages   B goods   C letters   D money

29 Ready Money

1 The first salesman showed the young man the door because he

A wanted to close the showroom
B thought that he had no money
C could not be polite to him
D did not have sixteen cars

2 The second salesman was polite and helpful when the young man

A took a bundle of notes out of his pocket
B paid for sixteen cars in cash
C examined an expensive car carefully
D asked for sixteen cars

30 A Dirty Suit

1 Mrs Field thought that her husband's suit was

A dirty   B light   C old   D nice

2 Mr Field thought that dark suits

A were nicer than light suits
B made him look older

C did not get as dirty as light suits
D did not show the dirt

31 A Day's Shooting

1 My uncle spent most of last Sunday

A looking tired and cross
B shooting birds
C arguing with a farmer
D shooting a cow.

2 My uncle had to pay £50 when he shot

A a farmer   B a cow   C a bird   D some birds

32 A Quiet Life

1 Mr Finch stayed in his cottage until

A too many visitors came to it
B he retired
C the summer holidays began
D the visitors stopped coming to it

2 Mr Finch bought another seaside house in order to have more

A peace   B money   C visitors   D work

33 Money Problems

1 I wanted to know

A what my brother did at the bank
B how long my brother had worked at the bank
C why my brother had decided to give up his job at the bank
D when my brother might become a bank manager

2 My brother did not enjoy

A working in pleasant surroundings
B keeping civilized hours
C counting his own money
D counting other people's money

34 A Spanish Holiday

1 The bullfight was very

A long   B uninteresting   C unusual   D impressive

2 The bull attacked the bullfighter while he

A was in the helicopter
B was coming down from the helicopter
C was showing his splendid costume to the crowd
D was trying to get his parachute off

35 An Unwelcome Visitor

1 Mrs Burbidge called at Mrs Carson's house to

A have a conversation with her
B offend Mr Carson
C use her telephone
D avoid her husband

2 Mrs Burbidge wanted her husband to

A get home from work
B be worried about her
C come to Mrs Carson's house
D stay at home

36 It Makes a Change

1 If a garden is well cared-for, it contains no

A rose bushes   B hedges   C weeds   D lawn

2 The gardener worked in his own garden during the week-end because

A it was very neglected
B gardening was his hobby
C he had no hobby
D he was paid for this work

37 A Message From Nowhere

1 Mrs Robinson was afraid that the guests had

A not received the sketch-map
B taken a wrong turning
C forgotten the dinner invitation
D had an accident

2 The guests telephoned Mrs Robinson from a village which

A was about ten miles away
B was not marked on the map
C had no name
D was called 'Nowhere'

38 Baby-sitting

1 How often had Carol done baby-sitting before?

A Once   B Several times   C Many times   D Not at all

2 While the little boy was watching television, Carol

A stayed in his room
B listened to the radio
C must have fallen asleep
D went to the living-room

39 Monday Morning

1 On Monday morning, nobody in the Crawfords' house is

A bad-tempered   B hungry   C cheerful   D in a hurry

2 The postman was cheerful because

A it was Monday morning
B it was a lovely day
C he did not live with the Crawfords
D he was not in a hurry

40 Look Where You're Going!

1 The workmen were sticking gold tape on the glass doors of the Palace Hotel in order to make them less

A dangerous   B impressive   C bright   D ugly

2 The unfortunate visitor was staring angrily at the glass door
because

A there were ugly bands of gold tape on it
B he could not walk through it
C it was broken
D he had just walked into it

41 The Balkan Express

1 When his grandfather opened the front door, the author was
so tired that he

A was unable to speak at first
B was reluctant to speak at all
C could not explain his appearance
D had to sit down before speaking

2 What did his grandfather conclude when he heard about the
author's journey on the Balkan Express?

A Young people don't know how to enjoy travelling nowadays
B Journeys on the Balkan Express are faster but less comfortable
nowadays
C The service on the Balkan Express is of low quality nowadays
D There are fewer musicians in Eastern Europe nowadays

42 Boys Will be Boys

1 Uncle Bill had sent a birthday present although

A it could not arrive on Tommy's birthday
B he was now living in America
C Tommy would soon be bored with it
D Tommy was only interested in stamps

2 The story is called 'Boys Will be Boys' because

A all fathers were once boys, and can still enjoy playing with
toys
B all boys soon get bored with toys when they are playing
with them
C boys usually want to open their birthday presents early
D Tommy kept his promise and did not open his present early

43 Well Worth the Money

1 Why were a lot of people standing beside the pond?

A They were watching the model boats on the water
B They were the owners of the model boats on the water
C A man had just begun to swim across the pond
D The pond was freezing, and they were hoping to skate on it soon

2 A man swam across the pond in order to

A attract attention
B break the ice
C have some exercise
D win a bet

44 Future Prospects

1 What sort of young men did the director *not* want to employ?

A Young men who were married
B Young men who liked ordinary jobs
C Young men who had been salesmen
D Young men who changed their jobs

2 Ernest's last question showed that he was

A not as young as he looked
B anxious to impress the director
C not as adventurous as he seemed
D anxious to get the job

45 Guests for Dinner

1 When did Mrs Alison regret inviting the Johnsons to dinner?

A When her husband said that they had not seen the Johnsons for years
B When she discovered that there was very little food in the house
C When her husband said that he had remembered to buy some steak
D When her husband went to open the boot of his car

2 The steak which Mr Alison had bought was likely

A to have become too bad to be eaten
B to be too small for four people
C to provide a satisfactory meal
D to have been stolen from his car

46 Back in Fashion

1 Millie decided to try the boots on when

A she saw them on display
B she heard their price
C the shop-assistant brought them
D the shop-assistant approached her

2 The story shows that white stockings

A have been in fashion more than once
B are always in fashion
C cannot be bought from shops
D can be worn by young people only

47 Blackmail

1 The boatman accepted Miss Merryweather's offer of $3

A unwillingly   B cautiously   C readily   D anxiously

2 What are we left to imagine Miss Merryweather did when the boatman stopped rowing and demanded $5?

A She paid him the sum he demanded
B She swam the remaining two hundred yards to the liner
C She refused to pay more than $3
D She shouted for help to the liner

48 The Ploughboy

1 The buyers' opinion of the picture was that

A it might be a masterpiece
B it was very cheap
C there was too much varnish on it
D it was not worth buying

2 Why did the author offer fifty pence for the picture?

A He thought it was a masterpiece
B He was sorry for the auctioneer
C He acted suddenly and without thinking
D He could not wait all day

Situations

1 *(Accepting invitations)* Your English teacher is talking to you, and invites you to his house. You would like to go to his house, so how would you reply to his invitation?

2 *(Advising)* A tourist asks, 'Which are the most interesting places to visit in this country?' Tell him two places he could visit, and what is interesting about them.

3 *(Agreeing)* A visitor is praising the view from your house. You have always liked the view too. What would you say?

4 *(Apologizing)* You are entertaining a visitor at your house, and offer him a drink. The visitor asks for whisky, but you do not have any whisky. Apologize for not having whisky, and offer your visitor an alternative drink.

5 *(Assenting)* You want to change some foreign currency at a hotel. The manager asks whether he may look at your passport. What would you reply?

6 *(Attracting attention)* You go to a bank to buy some foreign currency. The clerk behind the bank counter is copying some figures and seems not to have noticed you. What would you say to attract his attention?

7 *(Complaining)* You are at an airport, waiting for your suitcase to be brought from a plane. Some luggage is brought into the airport and an official announces that this is the luggage from your plane, but your suitcase is not among this luggage. What would you say to the official?

8 *(Congratulating)* A fellow student tells you that he has gained a place at an English university, where he will study engineering. You know that he has worked very hard to gain this place. What would you say to him?

9 *(Disagreeing)* Your host at a party remarks that all women drivers are dangerous. You disagree, but do not wish to offend your host. How would you reply to his remark?

10 *(Expressing appreciation)* Your English teacher, who has been very helpful to you, has told you that he will be retiring later this year because of age. What comments might you make on this news?

11 *(Replying tactfully)* A father shows you a painting by his seven-year-

old daughter, and asks your opinion of it. You think the painting is ugly and clumsy, but you can see that he is proud of it. What could you say, about the picture or about the artist, without flattering or offending the father?

12 *(Giving information)* You are going to meet a man whom you have never seen before, at a crowded station. He telephones you and asks how he will recognize you at the meeting-place. What would you say?

13 *(Giving personal details)* An official at a passport office asks for your place and date of birth, occupation, and country of residence. Reply to his enquiry.

14 *(Greeting)* You are at a party. A guest from abroad is introduced to you. What would be your first words to him, and what might you say after these?

15 *(Leave-taking)* Someone whom you have known for a short time says that he will be returning to his own country tomorrow. Wish him a safe journey, and ask him for his impressions of this country.

16 *(Making introductions)* Your pen-friend is going to stay for a week at your house. You meet him at the airport and bring him to your home. Introduce your sister to him, and him to your sister, and tell each something about the other.

17 *(Refusing)* You are eating a meal in a restaurant, and pause to look at the menu. The waiter approaches and asks, 'Shall I take your plate, sir?' What would you reply?

18 *(Requesting)* You want to know the time, but you are not wearing a watch. You approach a stranger who is wearing a watch. What would you say to him?

19 *(Thanking)* A visitor from abroad says that she will send you a book about her country when she returns home. What would you say?

20 *(Seeking information)* You telephone the nearest airport to enquire about flights to London. What questions might you ask?

21 *(Accepting invitations)* You are on a voyage and meet a man who makes his own wine. He gives you his address and says that you must try some of his wine, if ever you are in his home town. What would you say?

22 *(Advising)* A younger person tells you that he/she is thinking of buying a motor cycle. You do not think this is a good idea. How would you tell him/her this?

23 *(Agreeing)* A guest at a party says, 'The government ought to do something about the cost of food nowadays.' You want to express strong agreement. What would you say?

24 *(Apologizing)* You pick up the telephone and dial 212-6641. A voice says, 'Hallo! 212-6541.' What would you say?

25 *(Assenting)* A stranger asks you to help him with his car, which will not start. Express willingness to help him, and ask why the car will not start.

26 *(Attracting attention)* You walk into a shop. A bell rings, but no assistant appears. What would you say to summon an assistant?

27 *(Directing attention)* You are in a train, sitting in a *No Smoking* carriage. Another passenger lights a cigarette. What would you say to him?

28 *(Congratulating)* A neighbour has just passed the driving test, at the third attempt. You have always been confident of his/her ability to pass the test. What do you say now?

29 *(Disagreeing)* Someone says that success depends on luck. You believe that it depends on hard work. How would you express your opinion?

30 *(Expressing surprise)* A stranger sitting beside you in an aeroplane tells you that he is eighty years old. You are astonished, since you cannot believe that he is older than sixty. What would you say?

31 *(Expressing judgement)* A friend is showing you a very modern building in his/her home town. You are impressed by the appearance and setting of the building. What comments might you make?

32 *(Giving information)* You are standing at a bus stop, within sight of St Thomas's Hospital, which is about 400 metres away. Somebody asks you the name of the nearest hospital, where it is, and whether he will need to catch a bus to it. How would you reply to this enquiry?

33 *(Giving personal details)* You are being interviewed for a job with a travel firm. The interviewer asks how widely you have travelled. Tell him.

34 *(Greeting)* You are meeting a pen-friend at an airport. How would you greet him/her?

35 *(Leave-taking)* You are leaving a party, and are looking for your hosts. What would you say to them when you find them?

36 *(Making introductions)* You are walking in the street with a friend, and stop to talk with a fellow student of English. You realize that your friend and your fellow student do not know each other. Introduce them to each other, as informally as possible.

37 *(Refusing)* A friend suggests a visit to the local cinema. The local cinema is showing 'Castle of Blood', which you have already seen. What would you reply to your friend's suggestion?

38 *(Requesting)* You have found a seat on a train which is due to depart in 30 minutes. You want to ask another passenger to keep your seat while you buy a newspaper and some magazines. How would you do this?

39 *(Thanking)* A stranger helps you lift your case into a railway carriage. What would you say to him?

40 *(Seeking information)* You are in a shop and see a shirt on display, under a notice saying *Other Colours and Sizes Available*. You like the style of the shirt, but not its colour. Ask for a shirt in the same style, in your size and favourite colour.

41 An acquaintance asks, 'Are you interested in football? I've got some free tickets for the match on Saturday, if you'd like one.' You appreciate this invitation, and want to accept it: how would you reply to it?

42 A friend tells you that he is going to give up his job. You think that he is acting hastily and unwisely. What would you say?

43 It is mid-winter, and the sun is shining brightly. The postman calls at your house and remarks, 'Lovely weather!' What would you reply?

44 You are at a crowded party. You turn suddenly, and knock a glass from a girl's hand. Apologize to her, and offer to get her another drink.

45 You want to buy some socks, of any colour, at a local shop. An

assistant offers you some blue socks, and asks whether they will be suitable. What would you say?

46 You have locked your bicycle by the side of a road, and see a car reversing towards it. The driver does not seem to have noticed your bicycle. What would you shout to him?

47 You write 'Glass: Fragile' and 'Handle with Care' on a parcel, and take it to the post office. The assistant throws your parcel on a heap of other parcels. What would you say?

48 You are on holiday, and meet an old man who looks very healthy and cheerful. He tells you that he walks three miles before breakfast every day. What would you say on hearing this?

49 You have been waiting in a bus queue for half an hour, during which no buses have passed. You often have to wait a long time for buses, and are astonished when a woman in the queue tells you that the bus service is usually good. What would you say to her?

50 A fellow-student whom you know well tells you that she is going to marry another fellow-student whom you know well. How would you respond to this news?

51 You have been watching a play with a friend. You have fallen asleep several times during the performance, and afterwards your friend comments, 'What a boring play!' What comments might you make?

52 You have lost the key of your house and are attempting to climb through a window. A policeman approaches and asks what you are doing. Tell him.

53 You are the only witness of a road accident, and are telling a policeman about it. The policeman says that he will need to know your name, age, address, and present occupation. Give him the information he requests.

54 Your brother has fainted and is lying on the living-room floor. You have sent for a doctor, who has just arrived at your house. Greet him, ask him in, and tell him where your brother is.

55 You are leaving a library in which you have been studying all day. You will be returning to the library tomorrow. What would you say to the librarian as you leave?

56 You are the secretary of the Newtown Discussion Club. You have

invited a famous writer to speak to the club, and you go to meet him at the station. You recognize the writer and approach him. Introduce yourself to him and tell him what position you hold in the club.

57 A taxi-driver offers to take you to an airport five kilometres away for £5, which you consider much too high a fare. Decline his offer, and make it clear why you are declining it.

58 You are watching a film at a cinema when a lady wearing a tall hat sits in front of you. You can no longer see the film and there are no empty seats to which you can move. Ask the lady, politely, to remove her hat, explaining the reason for your request.

59 A neighbour helps you to repair your garden fence. What would you say to him when the work is finished?

60 You have a ticket for the eight o'clock show at the Globe Theatre. It is seven-thirty when you approach a policeman to ask the quickest way to the theatre. What would you say?

Possible appropriate responses

1. That's very kind of you/Thank you very much. I'd be delighted to come/I look forward to visiting you.

2. You could go to X. It's very beautiful/famous/old/picturesque. And you should visit Y. It's very . . .

3. It is beautiful, isn't it?/I'm very fond of it too.

4. I'm sorry. We don't have any whisky. Can I offer you something else?/What else can I offer you?/What about some . . . /a glass of . . .?

5. Certainly/Of course. Here it is/It's in my briefcase etc.

6. Hm! Hm!/Excuse me!/Could you help me, please? I want some foreign currency.

7. (Excuse me, but) I was on the plane, and my case isn't here/hasn't been brought.

8. (Very) well done!/Congratulations! You deserve it/this success.

9. I'm not sure whether I'd *entirely/fully* agree with you. *Some* women drivers may be dangerous, but not *all* of them, surely? Some men drive dangerously too.

10. I'm very sorry/sad to hear that. I'm very grateful for/I've very much appreciated your help. I hope you have a very happy retirement.

11. It's very interesting/unusual. Has she done/painted many like this? How old did you say she was/is she?

12. I'm . . . tall; I have . . . hair; I shall be wearing . . . /carrying . . .

13. I was born at . . . on . . . I am a/work as a . . . I live in . . .

14. How do you do, Mr X? (I'm) pleased to meet you/make your acquaintance. How long will you be staying here? Are you enjoying your stay here?/When did you arrive? etc.

15. I hope you have/I wish you/May I wish you a safe journey. How did you like/enjoy your stay here?/What do you feel about this country now?

16. X, may I present/introduce my sister, Y? She works at the . . . Institute. Y, this is X. We've been writing to each other for *n* years./He's just arrived from . . .

17. Not yet, thank you. I haven't finished/was just looking at the menu . . .

18. Excuse me, could you tell me the time, please?

141

19 Thank you. That's very kind/thoughtful/nice of you. I'll look forward to reading it.

20 Could you tell me the departure time of the next plane to London? Can you book me a seat on it? Could you tell me the fare? How long before departure do I have to be at the airport/check in at the airport? etc.

21 Thank you. I very much hope I'll be able to try some one day./I'd very much like to try some if I'm ever in . . .

22 I wouldn't, if I were you./I'm not sure that's a good idea./Motor cycles can be rather dangerous.

23 Yes they/it certainly ought to/should. I entirely agree.

24 Sorry. Wrong number.

25 Certainly I'll help./I'd be glad to help. What's wrong? (Have you run out of petrol?/Is the battery dead . . . etc.)

26 Hallo? Shop!/Service! Anybody there?/Is there anybody . . .

27 Excuse me, (but) this is a 'No Smoking' carriage. Would you mind not smoking (please)?

28 Well done!/Jolly good! I (always) knew you could do it/would pass.

29 I can't/don't agree. I think it depends on hard work rather than luck.

30 Well I never!/Good heavens!/I don't believe it! But you don't look more than . . .

31 It's a very beautiful/clever/tasteful design/piece of architecture. I like the way it fits into its setting.

32 (It's called) St Thomas's Hospital. It's over there/just down the road/ only a short distance from here. You can walk to it./You won't need to catch a bus.

33 I've been to . . . /I've travelled all over Europe./This year I went to . . . I'm afraid I haven't been to . . .

34 Hallo, X! How are you? Good journey/Had a good journey?

35 I'll have.to be going now. Thank you for a lovely party. I very much enjoyed it/It's been great fun etc.

36 You two haven't met/don't know each other, have/do you? X, this is Y. Y: X.

37 (Sorry, but) I'm afraid I've seen the film already.

38 Excuse me, can I ask you to keep this seat for me? I'm just going for/to buy . . .

39 Thanks. That's very kind of you.

40 Do you have a shirt like that/in that style, size 41/with a 41 cm. neck, in green/blue/purple etc.?

41 Yes I am very interested/I'm very keen on football. I'd like to see/go to the match. Thank you very much for asking me/It's very kind of you to ask me/offer me a ticket.

42 Are you sure that's wise?/Have you thought this over carefully?/I shouldn't do that yet, if I were you.

43 Yes it is, isn't it? Especially for the time of year.

44 I'm so/very/terribly/awfully sorry. It's so crowded. May I get you another (drink)?/Please let me get you another.

45 They'll be fine. The colour doesn't matter/isn't important.

46 Careful!/Look out!/Watch out! There's a bicycle (just) behind you!

47 Careful!/There's glass in that parcel! Didn't you read what I wrote on it?

48 That's excellent/very good/marvellous. No wonder you look so healthy/fit/well.

49 Well, *I* don't think it's very good./I can't agree. I'm always having to wait for buses.

50 What marvellous news!/Congratulations! I'm very glad/happy for both of you.

51 I certainly agree. I couldn't keep awake/was forever falling asleep/dropped off several times during it.

52 I live here/I live in this house/This is where I live (, officer). I've lost my front door key, so this is the only way in.

53 My name is ... I am ... years old. My address is/I live at ... At the moment I'm working in ... /as a ...

54 Good evening (etc.), doctor. Please come in./Do come this way. My brother is in here/in the living-room.

55 Good night. Thank you. I'll be seeing you tomorrow.

56 Good evening/afternoon, sir/Mr X. May I introduce myself? I'm .../ My name is ... I'm the secretary of the N.D.C.

57 No, thank you. I won't be going with you./I'll find another taxi. Your fare/charge is too high/much too high/ridiculous.

58 Excuse me, madam (but) can I ask you to/would you take your hat off? It's in my way./I can't see the film.

59 I very much appreciate/I'm very much obliged to you for all your help. Thank you very much.

60 Excuse me, officer, could you tell me how to/if I can get to the Globe Theatre by eight o'clock?

Answers to Multiple Choice Questions

Chapter One   1: 1 – D   2 – C   3 – A
                 2: 1 – C   2 – D   3 – B
                 3: 1 – A   2 – B   3 – C
                 4: 1 – A   2 – D   3 – B
                 5: 1 – A   2 – D   3 – C
                 6: 1 – C   2 – B   3 – B
                 7: 1 – D   2 – A   3 – D
                 8: 1 – D   2 – C   3 – B

Chapter Two   9: 1 – B   2 – C   3 – D
              10: 1 – D   2 – B   3 – C
              11: 1 – B   2 – A   3 – B
              12: 1 – C   2 – B   3 – A
              13: 1 – A   2 – D   3 – C
              14: 1 – C   2 – A   3 – B
              15: 1 – D   2 – D   3 – A
              16: 1 – C   2 – A   3 – B

Chapter Three   17: 1 – C   2 – C   3 – B
              18: 1 – B   2 – B   3 – D
              19: 1 – A   2 – D   3 – B
              20: 1 – A   2 – A   3 – C
              21: 1 – A   2 – D   3 – C
              22: 1 – D   2 – B   3 – C
              23: 1 – C   2 – A   3 – B
              24: 1 – B   2 – D   3 – D

Chapter Four   25: 1 – B   2 – A
              26: 1 – D   2 – B
              27: 1 – B   2 – B
              28: 1 – A   2 – C
              29: 1 – B   2 – D
              30: 1 – A   2 – D
              31: 1 – C   2 – B
              32: 1 – A   2 – A

Chapter Five	33:	1 – C	2 – D
	34:	1 – C	2 – D
	35:	1 – A	2 – C
	36:	1 – C	2 – B
	37:	1 – D	2 – B
	38:	1 – D	2 – C
	39:	1 – C	2 – B
	40:	1 – A	2 – D
Chapter Six	41:	1 – D	2 – C
	42:	1 – B	2 – A
	43:	1 – A	2 – D
	44:	1 – B	2 – C
	45:	1 – B	2 – A
	46:	1 – B	2 – A
	47:	1 – A	2 – A
	48:	1 – D	2 – C